CULTURE SKETCHES
CASE STUDIES IN ANTHROPOLOGY

CULTURE SKETCHES
CASE STUDIES IN ANTHROPOLOGY

HOLLY PETERS-GOLDEN
The University of Michigan

McGraw-Hill, Inc.

New York   St. Louis   San Francisco   Auckland   Bogotá   Caracas
Lisbon   London   Madrid   Mexico City   Milan   Montreal   New Delhi
San Juan   Singapore   Sydney   Tokyo   Toronto

This book is printed on recycled paper containing a minimum of 50% total recycled fiber with 10% postconsumer de-inked fiber.

1234567890   MAL MAL 909876543

ISBN 0-07-035954-7

The editor was Phillip A. Butcher;
the production supervisor was Phil Galea.
Malloy Lithographing, Inc., was printer and binder.

Cover photo: Adapted from David Lainé / Actuel.

For Marc, who was part of its first invocation,
and to Rebecca and Jenna, for whom it is a new lesson--
a more important truth than can be found in this, or any book:

You can achieve whatever you love
and will be loved whatever your achievements.

CONTENTS

PREFACE

Anthropology offers a unique perspective. Through its lens we can see, at once, both our kinship with all the rest of humanity as well as our uniqueness. Students peering through this lens for the first time often ask, "How are they the same as we are?" "How are they different?" It is usually with delight that they discover both striking similarities and surprising differences.

This volume is an introduction to nine societies, and each glimpse is brief and necessarily incomplete. It is my hope that any student who is intrigued will look further into the past and present lives of these people. The following chapters are aimed more at sparking interest than appeasing it.

The groups selected are all peoples whose traditional cultures are uniquely their own. Each have distinctive patterns and practices and often provide the prime illustration of important concepts in introductory anthropology courses: Azande witchcraft, Aztec human sacrifice, Tiwi pre-natal betrothal, Yanomamo warfare. Each has faced the challenge of an encroaching world, with differing results.

The complex Aztec empire is no more; Ojibwa culture flourishes. Kaluli music has been the vehicle for an aggressive campaign to prevent rainforest destruction. The isolation of the Tiwi was a salient feature in the development of much of their indigenous culture. Today, they are no longer isolated. They encourage tourism, while making sure younger generations are still taught to gather preferred "bush foods." Ethnographer Napoleon Chagnon, long associated with the Yanomamo, has pledged the rest of his career to their preservation. Nomadic pastoralists like the Basseri face challenges both from governments who think sedentary peoples are more "civilized," as well as from environmental analysts who are concerned about the impact of pastoralism and expanding deserts on agricultural lands. Resettlement and development, such as that undertaken among the Azande, cannot succeed if motivated solely by goals of industrial development but uninformed by indigenous culture.

Our world is more than ever a world of change. The exploration and promotion of cultural diversity has been embraced as a mission on some campuses, feared as a strategy of separatism by others, used as a weapon in other venues. As we are increasingly faced with a global culture, anthropology takes on an even greater responsibility to foster respect for differences in the face of change

Acknowledgments

Errors in fact and judgment in the text that follows are mine alone. I extend thanks, however, to those who share in whatever is most successful herein. To Conrad Kottak for his confidence; to Sylvia Shepard for her very able pencil; and to an electronic friend who kept me going daily when postmodernists threatened to take their toll.

Above all, my admiration and gratitude to Marc, Rebecca and Jenna -- fine foragers all--for their grace under pressure while the home garden was fallow.

Holly Peters-Golden

CULTURE SKETCHES
CASE STUDIES IN ANTHROPOLOGY

§ THE BEGINNING

There are those who can set broken bones. Only they, and people healed by them, can do this. The first of them long ago fathered a child, and the child had no arms and no legs. He was round, like a cooking pot. People saw him and knew he was a child of Mbori, the supreme being. The ancestor had a dream. In the dream he was told to burn the child, and this he did. He was told to take the child's ashes and mix them with oil; this he could use to heal broken limbs. The ancestor did all he was told to do. He used the ashes of the child born with no limbs, and created the clan of those who can heal the broken limbs of others.

INTRODUCTION AND HISTORY

The Azande people live in a large area in the center of Africa, in the southwestern Sudan, north of Zaire and to the east of the Central African Republic. This is an area of rolling hills

with abundant rivers and streams. On the banks of the waters grow tall trees, which provided shade in which to build homesteads. However, Azande fell victim to sleeping sickness spread by the tse-tse fly, which breeds in thick bush. Sudanese authorities, concerned about this exposure, forced them to relocate to concentrated settlements near roads. (The closeness of the houses in these new settlements was especially problematic. Formerly, structures along the river banks could be spread far apart; this was preferable to the Azande, who feared neighbors' potential witchcraft, which was only effective at close range.)

The peoples known collectively as the Azande are a melding together of what were separate clans in the past. In earliest times, the clans who lived along the banks of the waters were autonomous local groups. Clan disputes were settled within the families which comprised them. Disputes between clans were settled by elders from each. Azande history tells of a single individual who, through his wisdom and kindness, gained power within his own clan, the Avongara. Soon, under his able leadership, they became the dominant group. Moving eastward along the riverbanks, they conquered more than fifty other clans, and eventually amalgamated into one Azande group.. The history of the area is characterized by such invasions and warfare. (Reining 1966).

In the late nineteenth century, French and Belgian expeditions had set up military outposts in the Sudan; by the early twentieth century the Azande district was under British rule.

SETTLEMENTS

The individual homestead of each couple and their children is the focus of the economic system. The construction and maintenance of homes is a constant occupation, especially owing to the toll taken on them by weather, insects, animals, and fast growing vegetation.

Homes are built of mud and grass and framed on wooden poles and thatched with grass. (One addition to traditional Azande homes is the European introduction of doors fitted with hinges and locks.) In addition to this living space, each household unit had a granary for storing millet.. Houses were built around courtyards, which provided ideal places for gathering and conversation. These enclosed courtyards were seen as a window into the household life. Their upkeep was critical since they were seen as evidence of the responsibility or industriousness of their owners. Reining (1966:69) reports that his Azande informants would comment on the state of disrepair of their neighbors homestead, and "analyzed courtyards as reflections of the inhabitants." They did not exempt themselves from such scrutiny; he continues: "I received a number of apologies from the heads of households about the state of their courtyards, with full explanations for the deficiencies of which they were ashamed." (ibid)

The traditional courtyard arrangement appeared to have changed very little with European contact (Reining 1966), with the arrangement of each courtyard reflecting the composition of the household to which it is attached. Since each woman must have her own house and granary, polygynous households will have numerous homes and granaries around its courtyard. In a monogamous household, the average courtyard space is about 65 feet in its largest dimension. Households with more adult women may have yards of one hundred feet square. Courtyards belonging to the households of chiefs are double this size.

"Kitchen gardens" were planted adjacent to the courtyards. These were used for plants that didn't require large-scale harvesting or great attention. Pineapple, mango, papaya, and miscellaneous perennial plants used for meals immediate upon picking were found in these plots.

SUBSISTENCE AND MANUFACTURE

The Azande practice shifting cultivation (that is, no crop rotation, and incorporating a fallowing period), relying most on maize and millet, gourds and pumpkins, manioc and bananas, groundnuts, and beans. The tse-tse fly, problematic to animals as well as humans, makes cattle herding impossible. Whatever meat is consumed is secured through hunting. There is also a tradition of using forested area to gather plants which they do not cultivate. Dogs and chickens are the only domesticated animals.

The region has ample rainfall and many springs. These were a focus of Zande life, since they have usable water nearly year-round. Water for daily use was carried from stream to homestead and the washing, among other activities, was done at the river banks. In fact, the stream was central to Azande life in conceptual as well as practical terms. For example, distance is expressed by the number of streams between the points in question and the length of a journey is the number of streams crossed during travel. When asked about an exact location (such as an individual's birthplace) the answer will be the stream nearest that location. Given the centrality of the stream to the Azande, their relocation by the European administration caused major disruption in their cultural beliefs and practices.

The year consists of two seasons, one rainy and one dry. During the rainy summer, Azande cultivate their land. Although they have a long growing season and no frosts, the soil is not rich and insects are troublesome. As the hot, dry weather begins, crops mature and are harvested.

Hunting was most feasible in the dry season, when tall grasses had died or were burned, and when the harvest was over. During the rains, vegetation was too dense to allow necessary visibility

Since rivers were low during this dry season, fish were more accessible. Men employed baskets traps which they set in the rapids of rivers; women dammed the streams into small shallow pools, drained them by bailing, and collected the fish, snakes, and crustaceans that remained. Termites were a favorite food, and their high fat and protein content made them a nutritious part of the diet.

In pre-European days, each family was an independent unit of production. Iron tools and spears were used as bridewealth items, but in general there was no tradition of exchange between households, which consisted of a wife or wives, husband, their children, and other dependents (such as widowed elderly). There was a sexual division of labor, and both women's and men's work were necessary to maintain an efficiently functioning household. Construction and repair of the house and granary were the responsibility of men. The arduous task of maintaining the courtyard and its gardens fell solely to women. Wealth, possessed mainly by chiefs, was primarily in the form of foodstuffs; the tradition of destroying a person's worldly goods upon death left little chance of inheritance of property.

Azande have no tradition of occupational specialization. All manufacturing and craftswork were considered largely avocations, done by most. Woodworking and pottery, making nets and baskets, and crafting clothing out of bark were the most important of these skills.

SOCIAL AND POLITICAL ORGANIZATION

Kinship

Among the Azande, clan affiliation were not stressed at the local level. E. E. Evans-Pritchard (1971), the ethnographer most responsible for knowledge about the Azande, found, as he endeavored to gather genealogies, that "except in the royal clan, genealogical relationships between clansmen were very seldom known and usually quite untraceable."
(p. 14) Local groups, according to Evans-Pritchard, are more political units than anything else. He reports that his discovering members of the same clan living near one another is due as much to chance as anything else.

Chiefdoms

In pre-European times, the Azande were organized into a number of chiefdoms (sometimes called kingdoms), each of which was independent from another. The Avongara were nobility; in these days of Azande chiefdoms, it was to Avongara lineages that chiefs belonged. Despite the fact that chiefs of differing groups all belonged to the same clan, there was ongoing hostility and warfare between them.

Chiefs ruled their lands and peoples by appointing emissaries (usually sons, but always Avongara) who were sent out to manage various sections of their territories. Within these communities, commoners were deputized to aid in administration.

Chiefs functioned as military leaders, economic leaders, and political leaders. Unmarried men were recruited into groups that functioned both as warriors and laborers on the king's lands. The governors of the territories had gardens which were also worked by these troops. Both governors and chiefs collected food from the peoples in their domain (provincial governors sending on to the chief a portion of their tribute as well) to be redistributed. In addition to food, spears and other items (often payment for fines or bridewealth) were redistributed by the chiefs.

Warfare

Several miles of unsettled forest and bush were maintained between chiefdoms. Watch was kept on these borders by trusted sentinels who were designated to build there houses along these boundaries.

During the rainy season when grass grew tall and provided good cover, surprise attacks were made on these border sentries, usually ordered by the provincial leader. He undertook this action on his own, without permission granted from the chief. Counsel, however, was sought from a poison oracle, a process wherein poison is administered to an animal while questions are posed to the inhabiting spirit. The poisoned animal's behavior, as well as point at which it succumbed to the poison, were interpreted by those with such skills. Information was obtained concerning the most propitious days and place for the raid, the expected level of casualties, and which companies of warriors should be entrusted with the most dangerous duties. If the oracle indicated that the time was not right for victory, the plans were abandoned.

The oracle also designated a suitable time and place for the attack, and the proper individual to act as a spy. This individual was sent to report on as many aspects of the homestead to be raided as he could determine. Often the spy went under the pretense of visiting a relative or wishing to trade. The best time for a raid was on a feast day when men would be involved in the festivities, not likely to be armed, and quite likely to be drunk. To determine the exact day of the feast, the spy would plan his visit during the preparations for the festivities. Since beer was always brewed for the celebration, the spy could determine the feast day based on the stage of the brewing process.

A successful raid yielded tools, arms, food, and chickens, some of which was sent to the chief for redistribution. Whatever could not be carried off was destroyed. Huts and granaries were burned.

In addition to raids, there were larger mobilizations of war campaigns on a grand scale. These were ordered by the chief, after having consulted his own poison oracle, and might continue over a period of weeks. While knives and spears were used exclusively in raids, the introduction of rifles into these larger confrontations resulted in a shift from hand-to-hand combat to shots being fired from a distance. Only when ammunition was exhausted would those warriors yielding spears converge on the enemy.

Marriage

The traditional Azande system of marriage was greatly disrupted by European involvement. Administrators legislated broad changes, especially regarding bride payment, divorce, and age at marriage. Although many of these were ostensibly designed to improve the status of women, ethnographer Reining (1966:61-2) regards them rather as "an experiment in altering some aspects of a culture without providing for changes in values...[illustrating] the unpredictability of arbitrary cultural changes." Azande did not share the European view that marriage was especially disadvantageous to women, whom they never regarded as servile, despite administrative interpretation of their customs.

Traditionally, the instigation for marriage among the Azande comes from the potential groom. When a man wanted to marry a woman, he asked an intermediary to approach her father with his offer. Unless the suitor was deemed undesirable immediately, her father would discuss the matter first with his brothers and sisters, and next with the woman in question. If she was agreeable, the money sent with the intermediary was accepted.

Several days later, the suitor would visit his promised bride's parent, bringing gifts and demonstrating his respect. In turn, their daughter visited her suitor's home for a "trial period" of several weeks, after which she returned to her parents home to make her final decision regarding the marriage.

During the time spent in reflection by the woman, the groom-to-be consulted oracles to determine whether the marriage, should it occur, would be a happy one. If both oracle and woman regarded the match favorably, the bride's family traveled to the home of the groom, where the ceremony took place. The marriage was sealed with the installation of the new bride's own cooking hearth.

Reining (1966) describes traditional Zande marriage as a process which continues indefinitely over time, with a protracted payment of brideprice. A small part of the price was paid at the time of the marriage ceremony, but in reality a husband was always indebted to his wife's family. It was always his responsibility to help in his in-laws fields, and he had mortuary obligations in the event of a death in his wife's family.

The material payment of the agreed-upon brideprice was not, in fact, as important as the attitude and behavior of a husband to his wife and her parents (Reining 1966). If he was a gentle, loving husband and labored adequately for her parents, remuneration could be forestalled for years. This was often, in reality, the situation preferred by in-laws: it afforded them considerable influence over their daughter's husband. If the husband was not performing his duties adequately, the wife's parents might insist their daughter move back to their home, forcing the husband to negotiate with her parents for her return. Thus, the relationship of primary emphasis in marriage was that of a son-in-law and his wife's parents. In polygynous situations, men who had a good relationship with their in-laws often expressed the desire to marry his wife's sister because of the advantages of a good relationship with in-laws.

The topic of homosexuality in Azande culture has been regularly addressed, especially in the context of the unmarried warriors, who, during the several years spent living apart from women, had homosexual relations with the boys who were apprentice warriors. These practices, however, were no necessarily maintained as a lifelong pattern of sexual orientation. Generally after their experiences with so-called "boy-wives," the warriors entered into heterosexual marriages.

Less attention has been paid to Azande lesbianism, relationships that were often formed between co-wives. Although there is not a wealth of information concerning these practices, according to Evans-Pritchard (1970:1429), "All Azande I have known well enough to discuss this matter have asserted ...that female homosexuality... was practiced in polygamous homes."

Azande husbands felt threatened by such activities, yet could not stop them; thus, women usually kept the sexual nature of their friendships secret (Blackwood in Suggs and Miracle 1993). Two Azande women who wished to formalize their relationship could do so in a ritual that created a permanent bond (Evans-Pritchard 1970). In addition to assuring both the emotional and economic support of the partner, it has been suggested that this formalization (a ritual akin to Azande "blood brotherhood") may have both widened a woman's trade network and enhanced her position in the community. Blackwood (in Suggs and Miracle 1993) interprets these relationships as indicating that Azande men's control over women did not extend into the realm of activities between women.

RELIGION, BELIEFS AND EXPRESSIVE CULTURE

Missionaries settled in the Sudan beginning in the early part of the twentieth century, and attempted to draw on indigenous beliefs as a way to promote Christianity.

Mbori is defined by Evans-Pritchard (1937:11) as "a ghostly being to whom the creation of the world is attributed," Missionaries and government officials writing about the Azande attempted to create out of Mbori a deity which would fit their own tradition. Evans-Pritchard, however, warns against looking for religion, as organized elsewhere, in Azande culture. Mbori is not convincingly portrayed by the Azande as a god analagous to the Supreme Being as found elsewhere. They have no shrines to Mbori, and no materials used in worship. There is only one ceremony in which his name is invoked, and that is performed infrequently at best. When he attempted to pursue the topic of theology, and Mbori in particular, Evans-Pritchard found the Azande "bored by the subject ...and unable to express more than the vaguest ideas about him."

The trickster tales

One universal motif in folk literature appears to be that of the "trickster," and these tales are told among the Azande as well. To a large extent the tales serve to assert and affirm social rules. They provide examples of the consequences one can expect if moral dictates are not observed. They are always told for the benefit of children, to supplement didactic social training. They are designed to appeal to a young audience (although they often contain very adult themes, and are very much enjoyed by adults) by featuring a main character who possesses a child's curiosity and temptation to break the rules. Demonstrated in the behavior of the trickster are a child's propensity for imitation, the ramifications of overlooking part of a ritual, the dangers inherent in exhibiting behaviors or assuming a role in society which are inappropriate.

While there are many groups of trickster tales told among the Azande, the best known concern the adventures of a character named Ture. The stories focus on Ture's elaborate machinations as he attempts to secure what he is after, and ends in describing his great success or dismal failure. His wants are generally basics; he is often in pursuit of food, such as meat, termites, porridge, mushrooms, honey: the items most desirable in a Zande diet.

Ture's rashness often leads him to situations in which he must find a way to prevent his own death, often while in the form of a bird or animal. In many tales he is intrigued by either fire or water, sometime regarded as necessities, sometimes as playthings. Despite his need for everyday goods, he often pursues items of pure luxury: "salt to improve the taste of his food, a barkcloth which hums harmoniously as the wearer moves, and a means of opening termite mounds to provide him with a home instead of building huts." (Street 1972:83)

Ture often shows poor judgment and questionable values, striving for something only because it is novel, or belongs to someone else, rather than because it is of any use to him. Thus, when he learns that someone possesses the ability to remove his own intestines and clean them, he wants only to be able to learn to do the same; when he obtains a secret formula for putting out fires, he sets his own house ablaze just so he can extinguish it. As the latter example suggests, oftentimes Ture will create ends just for the ability to use the means. (Street 1972)

Once Ture has chosen a goal, he begins to set his strategy for its achievement. However, his strategies tend to ignore all social convention. He usually uses trickery or deception to get what he wants. However, his attempts to use others to satisfy his own needs usually end in failure.

Often Ture tries to use magical spells or rituals that are not his to use. Because he is not the rightful owner of the magic or ceremony, he is unable to obtain the results he seeks. (One is reminded of the troubles encountered by the "Sorcerer's Apprentice," who borrows his master's hat and attempts to perform his chores with magical assistance, only to be overwhelmed by the power he has unwittingly unleashed.)

Foe example, Ture overhears a discussion about how two sons found success in hunting after cutting off their dying father's toe. In his eagerness to try this formula for hunting success, Ture murders his father, buries the toe he has severed, and goes out to hunt. To his surprise, he catches very few animals, and most of his companions are killed during the effort. The formula, it turns out, is only effective when the toe is offered willingly.

In other instances, the formula backfires because it is in the wrong hands: Ture has obtained it under false pretenses, and he was not meant to have it. While Ture may overhear a strategy for success, or may be given the tool to implement a strategy, he often has to resort to trickery to get the desired secret or magic.

While tales end with a particular lesson--Don't attempt another's behavior without their skill, or, If you are greedy, your acquisitions will be too much to handle-- the Zande tales are more than merely moral examples. They employ themes common to many peoples. Evans-Pritchard suggests the tales "represent deeper psychological forces present in us all, those elements which we would like to give rein to but cannot because of the rules of society."(Street 1972:86)

The tales also endeavor to teach flexibility, since rules are not always functional in every situation. To instill the message that sometimes rules must be broken, Ture the trickster elaborates the middle ground between order and chaos, and moderation in the application of convention. Classically, trickster tales describe a society's boundaries and rules and assert its unique identity. If viewed from this perspective, the Zande tales help us to understanding their society as well as some broader tenets of human nature.

Witchcraft

The Azande are perhaps better known for their pervasive belief in witchcraft than for any other aspect of their culture. However, in his classic description of witchcraft among the Azande, Evans-Pritchard asks the reader to be aware "that the Zande cannot analyze his doctrines as I have done for him...It is no use saying to a Zande 'Now tell me what you Azande think about witchcraft' because the subject is too general and indeterminate...to be described concisely. But it is possible to extract the principles of their thought from dozens of situations in which witchcraft is called upon to explain happenings...Their philosophy is explicit, but it is not formally stated as a doctrine." (1937:70) (In such situations, an anthropologist endeavors to construct such a "doctrine" through fieldwork. The resulting product may look quite dissimilar from the indigenous view. (Barrett 1991).)

Witchcraft is thought to be an actual physical property residing inside some individuals, who may themselves be unaware of their power. It is inherited, passed from father to son and mother to daughter. Azande believe that if the soul of the father is more powerful, the child conceived will be a boy; if the mother's soul substance is greater, their child will be a girl. Thus, although every child is a product of both parents, each also has more of one particular parent's soul. And if that parent is a witch, inheriting this inherent power to do harm is inevitable.
Since this property is organic, it grows as a person grows. Therefore an older witch is a more dangerous witch. Children, whose witchcraft substance is so small, are never accused of major acts of harm (such as murder). They can, however, cause minor misfortunes for other children.

Unlike sorcery, which employs charms and spells, witchcraft is deployed by sheer willpower. Witches send the spirit of their own witchcraft entity to eat the flesh and organs of their intended victims. Thus a witch may be at home asleep at the time illness or injury occurs. It is the "soul of the witchcraft" that travels through the night . This substance cannot travel great distances, however, and it is for this reason that Azande feel more secure if they are able to live at a distance from their neighbors. The "short range" nature of witchcraft allows the perpetrator to be more accurately identified; all those beyond the limits of a witch's capabilities, even with evil intent, may be eliminated. If a person is taken ill while traveling, it is in the location that illness struck that the witch must be found.

The Azande believe that witchcraft is at the base of all misfortune, great or small. If a potter opens his kiln only to discover his pottery cracked, he intimates witchcraft; if a child stubs her toe at play, she suspects witchcraft; if a hunter is gored by an elephant, he lays blame for the injury squarely on a witch.

Azande entertain no concept of "accidental" death. People die only as victims of murder, whether committed by witches or by the magic of revenge reserved for retaliation against suspected witches.

Despite these convictions, Azande do not live in constant terror of witches. (Nanda 1991) In fact, Douglas (1980) reminds us that Evans-Pritchard's assessment of the Azande was that they were the happiest and most carefree peoples of the Sudan. "The feelings of an Azande man, on finding that he has been bewitched, are not terror, but hearty indignation as one of us might feel on finding himself the victim of embezzlement." (Douglas 1980:1)

Since a witch's motivation is not random, but rather envy or hatred directed at a specific person, a victim searches for a suspect among those with whom he has argued, or who may have cause to be jealous of him. How then can he identify his aggressor? For this, and other purposes, Azande consult a variety of oracles.

Oracles

The Azande consult oracles regarding a wide range of things about which they need information. They ask for guidance in planning a marriage, taking a journey, building a house, organizing a raid. In addition to whatever their current misfortune may be, they inquire about whether their health will be endangered in the future.

In pre-European times, Zande chiefs consulted oracles to confirm their military decisions, but chiefs were also charged with judicial duties. Every accusation was brought before the chief to adjudicate. To this end, he employed several people whose responsibility was to assist in the consultation of oracles. It has been said that the Azande belief in witchcraft is the supporting framework of their entire judicial system. (Mair 1974:221)

An oracle is a device for revelation. Among the Azande there are many from which to choose, with varying reputations for reliability. By far the most powerful is benge, the poison oracle, used by men alone. Its decisions are relied upon without question, and no undertaking of great import is attempted without its authorization. In attempting to convey its centrality, an Azande informant of Evans-Pritchard drew the analogy between the books of Europeans and the poison oracle of this own people. All the knowledge, guidance, memory and truth that are derived from trusted Western writings reside for the Azande within the poison oracle. Evans-Pritchard came to view it as less a ritual than a necessity:

"For how can a Zande do without his poison oracle? His life would be of little worth. Witches would make his wife and children sick and would destroy his crops and render his hunting useless. Every endeavour would be frustrated, every labour and pain would be to no purpose. At any moment a witch might kill him and he could do nothing to protect himself and his family. Men would violate his wife and steal his goods, and how would he be able to identify and avenge himself on adulterer and thief? Without the aid of his poison oracle he knows that he is helpless and at the mercy of every evil person. It is his guide and counsellor." (1937:262-3)

Despite this seeming indispensability, later ethnographers have pointed out that benge poison, expensive and difficult to obtain, was most likely an oracle available regularly only to men of wealth. This limitation may have acted both to engender social obligations and to grant power and prestige. Men who cannot afford the costly poison, or who do not possess the proper chicken to which the poison must be administered, ask a wealthier kinsman, or deputy of the chief, to consult the oracle on his behalf. It is their duty to oblige. It is older men who are likely to have the means to seek counsel from the oracle: this access to information gives them power over younger men. Not only can they ask the oracles about the intentions and behaviors of their juniors; they are also always supported in their decisions by the considerable weight of oracular authority, to which younger or poorer men have no direct access, and so cannot challenge. (Evans-Pritchard 1937).

The benge poison ordeal is an elaborate procedure, requiring great skill and finesse in both the administration of the poison and the posing of the questions. Poison is administered, by an expert in the task, to a small chicken. The expert must know how much poison is necessary, how much time should elapse between doses, whether it should be shaken to distribute the poison, how long and firmly the chicken should be held, and in what position. Each barely perceptible movement made by the bird is significant to the trained eye.

Once the poison has been administered the order in which questions are asked, whether they are phrased in a positive or negative frame, must all be determined by the questioner. The oracle is addressed as if it were a person. Every detail of the situation in question is explained, and each individual question may be embedded in five or ten minutes of speech. The benge poison shows its answer by responding through the chicken to the question, "If this is true, benge kill the fowl'" or "If this is not the truth, benge spare the fowl." Each answer is then tested by repeating the interpretation of its reply, prefaced with the question "Did the oracle speak the truth in saying..." (Mair 1974).

An oracle more readily available to all is the termite oracle. This is used as often by women as men, and even children may participate. Two branches are cut, each from a different tree. They are inserted together into a termite mound, and left overnight. The answer is indicated by which branch has been eaten. Though certainly less elaborate and costly than the benge oracle, consulting termites is a time-consuming affair, since only one question may be posed at a time, and one must wait all night long for the answer.

Least reliable but most convenient is the rubbing-board oracle, a device resembling a Ouija board, made of two small pieces of wood, easily carried to be consulted anywhere, at any time. One small piece of wood is carved with a handle, and is rubbed across the top of a second piece, fashioned with legs to stand on. Questions are asked as the wood is moved; as it sticks or catches, so the answer is revealed.

Accusing a witch

There are two distinct sorts of accusations of witchcraft: one in which illness or misfortune has occurred, the other after someone has died. These differ in both the function of accusing an individual, and the ramifications of being found guilty.

The aim of accusing a person of witchcraft in the former situation is to bring about some resolution to the conflict which induced the attack, and return the relationship to equilibrium . Speaking ill of a person, or even wishing someone injury, is ineffectual without a social tie: the curse of a stranger cannot do harm. Thus, a relationship with the accused it is a prerequisite for bewitchment . (An individual must be suspected, or else his or her name could not have been presented to the oracle for confirmation or denial of guilt.)

When the chicken dies during the benge poison ordeal, a wing is cut off, placed on a stick, and brought to the local deputy of the chief, telling him the name of the individual confirmed by the benge. A messenger, sent with the wing to the alleged witch, places it on the ground, and announces that benge has been consulted regarding the illness of the accuser. Usually this charge is met with denial of any ill intent. At the very least the accused pleads ignorance of harm derived from his or her own mangu, or witchcraft substance. As a demonstration of good faith, the alleged witch takes a mouthful of water, and sprays it over the wing. So doing, she or he beseeches the mangu to become inactive, allowing the victim to recover. The messenger reports these events to the chief's deputy.

In the event of a "murder," the aim is not pacification but revenge. Restoring amicable relations is clearly not possible; a post-morten accusation is an indictment leading to heavy compensation, sometimes paid with the witch's own life. Exacting such a toll permanently altered the relationship between the kin group of the victim and that of the accused. (McLeod 1972)

Witchcraft in its social setting

The Azande chiefdom is formally structured in a clear cut hierarchy, from the chiefs at the top through their deputies, armies, local governors, and ending with individual householders. Built into this structure was the elimination of most opportunities for unequal competition: that is, chiefly lineages did not compete with those lesser, nor did the rich with the poor, or parents with their children. As Douglas (1980) has observed, accusations of witchcraft arose only in those social situations which fell outside of the political structure. Thus, co-wives might accuse each other, as might rivals in other arenas. Since witches could be unintentionally dangerous, their mangu could be set into motion by understandable resentments and jealousies. The accusation and eventual demonstration of remorse set these ill-feelings to rights. Events that can be explained by an individual's lack of technical skill (such as the shoddy work of an inexperienced carpenter) by personally motivated actions are not likely to be involved in the realm of witchcraft. As Parsons (1969:195) observes, one can imagine many motivations for a person to claim that witchcraft was at the root of their adultery, but this would result in ridicule,

"because everybody knows witches don't do that."

Witchcraft beliefs can function effectively as a way of managing the anxiety resulting from random misfortune. This is evidenced by the prominence given to illness and death as occasions for witchcraft accusations.

Witchcraft as social control and leveling mechanism

Witchcraft may serve as an effective agent of social control. The lengthy process involved in making a accusation acts to forestall hasty and emotional confrontations. Charges must have group support behind them and are not leveled carelessly.

An individual's behavior can be guided by the knowledge that wrongdoing might likely result in retaliatory witchcraft. Additionally, cognizance that jealous or hostile behavior might place one in a position of being suspect should misfortune occur might lead one to be quite circumspect. Wishing to be neither suspect nor victim, Azande possess, in witchcraft, both an effective sanction against socially disruptive behavior and a vehicle for handling hostility.

Because an individual with great wealth is likely to engender the jealousy of others and the attendant bewitchment, Azande are not likely to attempt to outproduce. It is in this way that witchcraft acts as a levelling mechanism, indirectly keeping wealth balanced

The "logic" of Azande witchcraft

The attribution of the cause of all misfortune to witchcraft may seem extreme. In fact, Evans-Pritchard himself engaged in lively debate with informants who described as witchcraft events that seemed to him the result of entirely "natural" phenomena. He eventually recognized that they did, in fact, have a very clear understanding about the contribution of the natural world to their misfortune. When Evans-Pritchard suggested to a boy, whose foot had been injured when he tripped over a tree stump, that a witch could not possibly have placed the tree stump in his way, the boy agreed. He recognized that nature had contributed the tree stump, and, further, that the tree stump had cut his foot. His evidence of witchcraft was simply that despite his vigilance in watching out for tree stumps, as well as his safe passage on that same path hundreds of other times, this time he had been injured. This time, there was witchcraft.

Along these same lines, when a granary collapsed, injuring several people who had been sitting in its shade, Azande saw no contradiction in their dual assertions that termites had eaten at the legs of the building, resulting in its collapse and that witchcraft was responsible. They further admitted that no witch had "sent" the people underneath the granary in order to trap them: it was afternoon, and they were merely seeking shade. While we would call this series of events coincidence, or perhaps "being in the wrong place at the wrong time," Azande are able to form an explanatory link between these events. That link is provided by witchcraft.

During his stay in the Sudan, Evans-Pritchard witnessed the suicide of a man who was angry with his brothers. Although his despair over his conflict was well known, and when his body was found hanging from a tree, all readily acknowledged that he had, in fact, hanged himself, the cause of death was witchcraft. At Evans-Pritchard's behest, an Azande friend explained: "...only crazy people commit suicide; if everyone who was angry with his brothers committed suicide there would soon be no people left in the world; if this man had not been bewitched he would not have done what he did do." (1937:71)

It is once the supernatural premise--that people have witchcraft substance in them, and can harm others with it--is granted that the Azande argument becomes logical.

These beliefs concerning witchcraft endure today, with some modifications.

Resettlement has forced them to accept living in closer quarters, depending upon screens to keep them out of neighbors' view, if not their reach. When asked about fears concerning the proximity of witches, Azande report that they feel able to relocate should misfortune occur. This would remove them from any nearby threat.

EUROPEAN DEVELOPMENT AMONG THE AZANDE

In recent years there has been widespread resettlement of the Zande people, as well as encouragement to participate in agriculture and industry which is profitable to European administrators (chiefly cotton production). Planners believed they could improve the lot of the Azande, who, it was thought, would be grateful for the introduction of more "modern" comforts and luxuries. The introduction of money and wage labor acted to weaken kinship ties by obviating the need for kin to work together outside the household. Young men and women could more easily leave their parents homes and set up their own households with income from wages paid by Europeans.

The most detrimental feature of the resettlement plan was the arbitrary assignment of individuals to plots of land. This action failed to take into account the Azande's desire for mobility and flexible living arrangements. Tensions were engendered between resettled people which were counterproductive to the developers' wishes to create, through resettlement, a stable workforce.

Reining (1966), in his assessment of an Azande development project to bring the cotton industry to the Azande region of the Sudan, concludes that it " proved that it is possible to establish an industrial community in the center of Africa, if cost is no object, and that the Azande could adjust...and produce large amounts of cotton when interested in doing so. But [it] also proved that many things cannot be done. Some of its weaknesses--especially those in ecology, social organization, and communication--will be found ...in other widespread attempts at economic aid and community development." (p. 231)

REFERENCES

BARRETT, R.A.
1991   Culture and Conduct.
            Belmont: Wadsworth.

BLACKWOOD, E
1993   Breaking the Mirror: The
            Construction of
            Lesbianism and the
            Anthropological Discourse
            on Homosexuality. in
            *Culture and Human
            Sexuality*. D. N. Suggs
            and A.W. Miracle,
            eds.Pacific Grove:
            Brooks/Cole.

DOUGLAS, M.
1980   *Purity and Danger*.
            London: Routledge &
            Kegan Paul.

EVANS-PRITCHARD, E. E.
1937   *Witchcraft, Oracles and
            Magic among the Azande*.
            Oxford: The Clarendon
            Press.

EVANS-PRITCHARD, E. E.
1970   (original 1929) Witchcraft
            amongst the Azande. in
            Witchcraft and Sorcery.
            M. Marwick, ed.
            Baltimore: Penguin
            Books.

EVANS-PRITCHARD, E. E.
1971   *The Azande: History and
            Political Institutions*.
            Oxford: The Clarendon
            Press.

MAIR, L

1974   *African Societies*.
            Cambridge: Cambridge
            University Press.

MCLEOD, M. D.
1972   Oracles and Accusations
            among the Azande. in
            Zande Themes. A.Singer
            and B. V. Street. Oxford:
            Basil Blackwell.

NANDA, S.
1991   *Cultural Anthropology*.
            Belmont: Wadsworth.

PARSONS, A
1969   *Belief, Magic, and
            Anomie*. New York: The
            Free Press.

REINING, C.C.
1966   *The Zande Scheme: An
            Anthropological Case
            Study of Economic
            Development in Africa*.
            Evanston: Northwestern
            University Press.

STREET, B.V.
1972   The Trickster Theme. in
            Zande Themes. A.Singer
            and B. V. Street, eds.
            Oxford: Basil Blackwell.

§ THE BEGINNING

The world before had existed not once, but four times, and these were the Ages of the Suns. Water, earth, wind, and fire each had their reign. Each ended in disaster.

The first people were formed of ashes, and when the water came they were carried away and changed into fishes. In the next sun there were giants, and tigers waited for dark to devour them. The giants were weak despite their size, and warned one another: do not fall. But they fell, and when they fell, they fell forever. During the third sun, the rain was made of fire, and all burned. The fourth sun was the wind, and swept everything away. The people became monkeys and fled to the mountains.

Now it is the fifth sun. New people are created from the remains of the old. Quetzalcoatl will restore them, and feed them maize. (León-Portilla 1992)

AZTEC HISTORY

Journey to the Valley of Mexico

The people referred to as Aztecs called themselves Mexica. Arriving in central Mexico as nomads in the thirteenth century, they had risen to a position of political and military power by the time the Spanish arrived in 1519. With Tenochtitlan as the capital of their empire, they had forged alliances with neighbors to the east and west.

Mexica migration into the Valley of Mexico began from Aztlan in the northwest some two hundred years before their eventual arrival. As they marched south, they were met with great hardship, expelled from each place they attempted to settle. Throughout the Valley of Mexico, elaborate states were already flourishing. The peoples settled here had complex and specialized technologies, including a sophisticated system of irrigation which afforded them a variety of crops in abundance. In addition, they possessed intricately organized social and economic systems. The nomadic Mexicas were not welcomed in their attempt to seek out unsettled land.

Their arduous trek was plagued with dissension from within (Berdan 1982) and treachery from without. Evidence for internal rebellion is found in numerous accounts of their journey. Along their route whenever they stopped they constructed a temple for Huitzilopotchtli, the most revered of the deities, who provided guidance on their exodus. Among the ceremonies conducted at these sites were human sacrifices, for which the Aztecs have come to be known. Many explanations have been offered for the various sacrificial occasions in Aztec culture. Berdan (1982) suggests that those performed en route to their permanent home may have served the purpose of eliminating the dissenting among the group, who were agitating to remain where they were and not continue on their journey as Huitzilopotchtli decreed.

Exemplifying the rejection they experienced from others is the response to Mexica request of asylum from the ruler of Calhuacan. Their petition to settle in his kingdom was met with the granting of territory he knew to be infested with poisonous snakes. He was sure this would put an end to these "undesirable Mexicas" (León-Portilla 1992:31). Instead, they roasted the snakes, ate them, and triumphed. Apparently surprised at the Mexica tenacity and impressed by their military skills, those living in the area engaged the Mexica as their mercenaries. Coupled with some of their more aggressive customs, these martial skills elicited both fear and hatred from surrounding peoples. When a ceremony to dedicate the king's daughter as a goddess resulted in her death and flaying, the Mexica were forced to flee once more.

Tenochtitlan

Camping by the marshy shores of Lake Texcoco, they were instructed by Huitzilopotchtli to look for the sign that would at long last indicate to them the site of their final destination. They saw this sign--an eagle resting atop a prickly pear cactus--and knew they had reached the end of their difficult journey. They named the place Tenochtitlan, "the place of the fruit of the prickly pear cactus." (Berdan 1982)

The founding of Tenochtitlan in 1325 ended their wandering, but certainly not the struggle of the Mexica people. Both the physical and the sociopolitical environment presented enormous challenges. Tenochtitlan was built on an island on the western side of Lake Texcoco. While the lake provided fish and aquatic birds, ease of canoe transportation, and chinampas cultivation (so-called "floating gardens"), the site was not without disadvantages. Chief among these were the lack of wood and stone for use in construction and the threat of floods.

Sociopolitically, the Mexica had established themselves on the boundaries of existing powerful states. Their history of overcoming adversity stood them in good stead. They attached themselves to the ruling Tepanec empire and began to strengthen themselves by forging alliances through marriage.

Within the Tepanec empire, it was the ancient Toltec line of nobility who were viewed as legitimate rulers. The first Mexica ruler in Tenochtitlan married a woman from a royal line, assuring the offspring of this union (and their descendants) legitimate claim to Toltec heritage. The ruler's son further cemented this bond by making a similarly politically astute marriage. Relations between the Mexica and the Tepanec ruler were cemented by these ties (especially after the birth of a son to the Mexica ruler and the Tepanec lord's granddaughter), and the Mexica became allies rather than subordinates.

As a result of these shifts in power relations, the Mexica population became increasingly socially stratified. Rulers headed a class of nobles who claimed private ownership of land and the prerogative to hold important public offices. The largest portion of the Mexica population remained commoners, who worked the land and fought the battles. Between these classes of commoners and nobility were occupational specialists: merchants and craftspeople. (Berdan 1982)

While attending to war strategy and political power occupied the nobility, the average Mexica devoted themselves to the construction of temples and houses, and chinampas cultivation. The latter was of crucial importance, not only because filling their own subsistence needs afforded the Mexica some degree of autonomy, but also because it was a key to necessary expansion.

The Mexica population grew rapidly, due in part to immigration supplementing natural growth. As conditions became crowded, people left Tenochtitlan to settle adjacent islands. Successful chinampas cultivation provided a consistent resource base, allowing the Mexicas to conquer other groups and exact tribute. (Berdan 1982)

During this time, a powerful Mexica military force was being assembled. Joining with two neighboring allies, the Triple Alliance was formed, successfully dethroning the Tepanec empire and beginning the most dramatic expansion in the history of Mesoamerica.

ECONOMIC ORGANIZATION

Tenochtitlan was connected to the mainland by three raised, paved roadways. In the center of the city were eight or nine walled-off ceremonial sites, surrounded by the palaces and homes of the nobility.

Palaces were elaborate edifices with several buildings and courtyards. Housed in the palaces were artists, craftworkers, servants, nobles, and government officials. Structures included a courthouse, warrior's council chamber, storage space for acquired tribute (and housing for those who looked after it), chambers for singers, dancers, and instruction of various kinds. Occupants and daily visitors to the place numbered over a thousand.

Cities of this scope rely on material support. Central and southern Mexico was a place of environmental diversity, with intensive production and economic specialization resulting in a surplus of goods. The Valley of Mexico, heart of the Aztec empire, was ideally suited to provide its inhabitants with resources for food, clothing, housing and tools.

Subsistence

The Aztec empire was built on agriculture, and at the core of this agriculture was maize. It formed the mainstay of the diet in various forms, and could be successfully grown in both the high plateaus and the tropical lowlands. This success was largely climate dependent: maize thrives best where rains are concentrated in the summer, as they are throughout Mesoamerica. Summer rains allow early planting and harvest before early November frosts. The Valley of Mexico yielded one crop of maize per season; in the lower elevations, two crops were possible. It has been suggested (Berdan 1982) that Aztec conquest of the more temperate zones outside the valley may have been spurred by the desire for a reliable source of maize.

In the middle of the fifteenth century central Mexico experienced severe famine. Within fifty years the Triple Alliance had secured control of maize production in widespread ecological zones where maize could be harvested at different times. This acted to assure that the effects of famine were less disastrous to the Mexica. Also helping to offset hunger were ritual feasts given by Aztec rulers in honor of the goddess of maize: prestations of food to people in need helped them through difficult seasons.

Its centrality in subsistence earned maize a glorified position in Aztec culture. Hardly a mere foodstuff, it was intimately involved in Mexica daily life. People personified maize, and addressed it with reverence as it was planted. Poetry, hymns, sayings, and stories all deified the crop and linked people metaphorically to it. An individual speaking out of turn or imprudently was "like an ear of maize split open;" one who had gained great prestige was said to have "reached the season of maize."

Also widely cultivated throughout the Aztec empire were beans, chiles, squash, maguey, and a host of other fruits and vegetables. From cactus were produced alcoholic beverages, fibers for clothing, medicinal remedies, and sewing needles. In the tropical lowlands, cotton and cacao (chocolate) were additionally cultivated.

In those areas of the highlands not conducive to irrigation, most employed systems of fallowing, supplemented by terracing and crop rotations. In shallow lakebeds or flatter stretches, floodwater irrigation was used. Chinampas agriculture was by far the most intensive irrigation agriculture strategy. Mud and vegetation was piled in shallow portions of a lake. Posts were attached to secure the plot until the roots of willows planted at the sides and corners could act as anchors. In the areas outside the densely populated urban centers, families cultivated chinampas plots that not only supported their own needs but also yielded enough surplus to be exchanged in the city for specialized goods and services. This funneling of surplus food into the urban area of Tenochtitlan most likely provided the subsistence to those specialists in service to the nobility, who could not be provided for by the smaller more crowded chinampas in urban areas.

Cultivation was usually combined with gathering wild foods, hunting, and fishing. Medicinal herbs were of great value, as were peyote and mushrooms. These, along with fruits available predominantly in the lowlands, were in great demand at the marketplaces.

Hunting held an esteemed place among the Mexicas, dating back to their nomadic past. In addition to providing food, fur, and skin, animals were hunted to supply the empire's zoos. Meat from land animals such as armadillo, deer, rabbits, boars and opossum were all part of the regular diet, and hunted with snares or bow and arrow. The lakes provided plentiful fish, reptiles, and crustaceans. Duck, quail, pheasant, and partridge were hunted by the lakeshores, and were valued as much for their feathers as for their flesh.

The Mesoamerican food producing environment allowed both intensive and varied agriculture. This yielded two important consequences: first, it led to specialization in production. Those residing by the lakeshore could devote themselves entirely to fish and waterfowl; farmers in drier areas could specialize in products derived from cactus. Second, these specialized systems of food production resulted in enough of a surplus to allow many people to instead direct their talents to professional occupations other than agriculture.

Occupational specialization

In the urban centers of Mexico, craft manufacture was highly elaborated, with entire residential sections of town home to painters, goldsmiths, silversmiths, featherworkers and sculptors. While their creations were held in high regard by the entire Aztec population, these products were available only to the nobility. Consequently the artisans themselves enjoyed great prestige, organized into exclusive guilds which had privileged relationships to the state. They resided separately, and had access to both temples and schools reserved especially for them. Featherworkers appear to have been especially esteemed, creating headdresses, fans, and costumes for nobility and the highest ranking military personnel. Stoneworkers and metallurgists had similar exclusive residences and were granted political clout.

The craft practiced most widely was weaving, an endeavor reserved only for women, and pursued by women of all classes. While every girl and woman learned to spin and weave cloth, the materials with which they worked and the garments they produced varied greatly by the status of the weaver. Women of the lowest ranks produced simple goods for household use; noble women engaged in producing the elaborate ceremonial capes, using the finest cotton, rabbit fur, and feathers.

Clothing served the dual purpose of being both utilitarian and identifying the class of the wearer. Commoners were bound to wear garments made from only the coarsest fabrics. Nobility had no apparel forbidden to them, but usually chose to exercise their privilege and wear the most elegant of vestments. Within the highest class, more decorative clothing signaled greater wealth.

Political, military, and religious specialists also emerged, as did "a host of miscellaneous occupations," (Berdan 1982:34) a situation to be expected in such a complex society. Astrologers, midwives, scribes, and prostitutes are counted among these.

Trade and Exchange

Markets were the economic link between different regions of production, the political focus for gossip and information, and the social setting for most neighborhood interaction.

The outdoor marketplace was the hub of every community, providing a meeting place for people of every age and social status to talk and share news, as well as conduct business. Wares reflected the local environment in terms of items abundantly available; larger markets trafficked additionally in luxury items. Barter was typically the medium of exchange, but money in the form of cacao beans and cotton cloaks was common. Less usual were bells, beads, and quills filled with gold dust.

Textiles which were bartered and sold in the marketplace functioned as items of trade, religious offerings, marriage payments, decoration, and cremation cloths, among others uses. Trade was carried on by all members of the society, whether they were professional artisans or individual agriculturalists. Families routinely sold their surplus in public marketplaces. These small-scale producers were vendors in the marketplaces and traded their wares to all passersby. Professional merchants were important on an entirely different scale. Their status afforded them political importance, but also economic sway: the luxury items they produced were of paramount importance for the nobility to display as symbols of their status.

Specialization required a fairly sophisticated system of exchange that began in the marketplace. Distribution of goods was also accomplished through tribute and trade routes, numerous enough for individuals to secure a wide range of goods. Trade, both foreign and domestic, forged political ties along with the economic.

The tribute collected from conquered regions provided revenue in exchange for the promise of protection. A wide variety of goods were given in tribute, with the majority typically being the most locally accessible items. Those provinces nearest the Triple Alliance capital cities most often provided surplus agricultural goods, textiles, and wood and paper products. Distant provinces, located in different ecological zones, provided more exotic goods, which might include rubber balls, chocolate, jade, quetzal feathers, and liquid amber.

It was the commoners on whom the burden of tribute fell most heavily. Cultivators struggled to amass the tremendous amount of food demanded, and artisans turned over the most valuable items they wrought. For those living in provinces on the outskirts of the empire, little more than offers of future protection were given in return. Those closer to the capitals could hope to reap some of the subsistence goods; and as they more often paid tribute in labor than in goods, they were likely to be working on city-improvement tasks that ultimately were of benefit to them.

The enormous stores of tribute were used to sustain the large and complex bureaucracy of the empire; to finance the military; to support the royal palaces; to bestow gifts; and to promote foreign trade.

SOCIAL ORGANIZATION

Class structure

The Aztec empire was a complex, stratified society with social organization guided by the principles of hierarchy and heterogeneity (Berdan 1982). Although ones position at birth (ascribed status) most circumscribed the positions to which one could aspire, there was room for upward social mobility through accomplishments (attained status).

The most basic social distinction existed between the commoners and the nobility, and these were conferred at birth. Initially, membership in the nobility demanded the ability to trace ones ancestry back to the first Mexica ruler. However, as Berdan (1982) points out, the practice of polygyny and the fact that noble status was passed through both males and females led to an exceedingly high number of people who could lay claim to noble birth. By the early sixteenth century, more stringent rules for reckoning legitimate noble descent were put into place.

Rigid dress codes made status differences readily apparent. Commoners wore simple clothes and their cloak had to end above the knee. The nobility alone could wear headbands, feathers, gold armbands, and jewels in their lips, ears, and noses. Only the ruler and his second-in-command could wear sandals.

Housing was also a status marker. Only those of noble rank could build two story houses. When visiting the palace, commoners knew which rooms were open to them, and which were reserved for nobility. Separate courthouses were maintained for passing judgment on individuals of different classes. In these courthouses, nobility were judged more severely than commoners. For example, a commoner charged with public drunkenness was punished by having his head shaved, while a nobleman would be put to death for this same offense. There are reports of rulers sentencing their own children to die for committing adultery.

Of course, the more far-reaching differences between classes were economic and political. Ownership of land, access to public and religious office, and control over important resources were tied to social class.

Along with the rights and privileges accruing to (or denied to) each status, there were accompanying expectations of behavior and lifestyle.

The provincial rulers formed the top rank of the nobility. Their power was determined by the size of their territory. Those whose dominion was smaller or less central paid tribute to those who ruled the Triple Alliance capitals, Tenochtitlan, Texcoco and Tlacopan. The responsibilities of all rulers included collecting tribute from commoners, organizing military expeditions, sponsoring religious feasts, and the ultimate adjudication of legal disputes which could not be settled by the courts. Despite the fact that this status was bestowed by birth, the personal qualities of an individual ruler often greatly influenced his ability to govern successfully. The ideal ruler was one who acted as a protector and unifier, assuming the burdens of leadership as well as its rewards. Although succession usually passed to brother or son, this was often contingent upon personal achievements.

Chiefs formed the rank below rulers, and this status was usually granted to those who had demonstrated superior military valor. Most chiefly duties involved military leadership, either advisory or on the battlefield, or that of judge.

Sons of nobility were a recognized class, to whom rights and privileges afforded nobility accrued, and who could expect to ascend to prestigious posts, even if they did not themselves become rulers or chiefs.

The provincial nobility were largely concerned with agricultural and not urban issues, as might be expected. The administration of land and water rights were of greater import than the military, manufacturing, or trade.

The commoners made up the largest portion of the population. They worked the land, filled the lowest ranks of the military, and paid tribute. They were not, however, a homogeneous group. For example, commoners had varying access to land; some of the more well off had tenant farmers.

Commoners were organized into calpulli, a territorial unit based on kinship, literally meaning "big household." Nuclear families, independent of one another, were strongly favored, but extended households were very common (León-Portilla 1992). Earlier, before the rise of large urban areas, assemblages of households who reckoned descent bilaterally from an apical ancestor constituted a calpulli. As these groups settled, calpulli came to be the designation for a ward, or barrio. Sometimes these were groups of occupational specialists. In every case, each calpulli had its own temple, in which the group recognized a particular calpulli deity, and through which they maintained a shared identity. In addition, calpullis had their own school, dedicated largely to martial training. Calpulli themselves were socially stratified, with a headman, council of elders, and members who worked the land.

There were also "serfs" (rural tenant farmers) and "slaves" in Mexica social structure. Each of these classes of individuals was drawn from the stratum of commoners. People who were homeless, through economic need or through warfare made up the majority of these ranks. Individuals also sold themselves or family members into slavery for subsistence needs. Those unable to pay debts, tribute, or fines also ran the risk of succumbing to this fate. This was, in almost all cases, an acquired status: children of serfs or slaves were born into freedom.

Kinship, marriage, and family

Early reports emphasize kinship as the single most important principle in Mexica society: the lineage was referred to as "the set of cords that unite humans." (León-Portilla 1992:127) The Mexica reckoned descent bilaterally, as did most indigenous central Mexican peoples. Both mother's and father's brother were called "uncle," and both mother's and father's parents were called "grandparents." Relative age, more than lineality, was a factor in determining social relationships. Distinctions were made between ones older and younger siblings. Beyond one's own generation, however, distinctions continued to be made on the basis of sex in ascending generations (parents, grandparents) and the generation below (son, daughter) but not beyond (all grandchildren were referred to by the same term, regardless of sex). Kinship rules functioned as the guiding factors in marriage, residence, and patterns of inheritance.

Among the nobility, the primary aim of marriage was to strengthen or forge powerful political ties. Ruling houses of neighboring capitals often maintained their relationships through such marriages for hundreds of years on end. Typically, this pattern allowed for the manipulation of inheritance to the satisfaction of both ruling families. The nobility were polygynous, but the commoners were not. This practice produced many individuals who aspired to relatively few positions. Inheritance was not based solely on the dictates of kinship; achievement often tipped the scale in the awarding of titles to one of many "rightful" pretenders. Unlike titles or official positions, land and houses could be divided among several heirs.

Cross-cousin marriage was common, and class endogamy appears to have been the rule. The calpulli, too, tended to be endogamous, which acted to keep resources within a guild, in the case of calpulli organized by occupational specialty.

Marriages were arranged for youths by their parents. When they decided a child was of marriageable age, parents prepared a feast of tamales and chocolate to which all the youth's teachers were invited, and at which they ritually discharged their student from their care. There is little evidence that the youth's own wishes were taken into consideration in the search for a suitable mate. Older women of the community served as brokers for the match. Once married, it was the primary responsibility of the new couple to join or establish a household, and have children.

One feature of kinship systems in which descent is reckoned bilaterally is the usual absence of strict post-marital residence rules, and this was the case in Mexica society. Actual residence patterns vary by location. In some areas, nuclear families predominated; in others, joint households were more common. Often the incentive to form either a nuclear or joint household would be provided by the demands of land tenancy and agricultural and subsistence needs. Flexibility in residence patterns assured that family structure could be altered to adapt to available resources.

Aztec life and customs

The ideal attributes of a Mexica citizen was to be moderate and discrete in all pursuits. Men were expected to serve as providers and teachers, tending most assiduously to the world outside the household. Women operated in the domain of the household, weaving, educating small children, and overseeing the efficient conduct of the family. Children were expected to show parents respect and obedience.

Young children were expected to be dependent, and little was asked of them. By the age of five or six, greater expectations were placed on all children. These were aimed at instilling the virtues of honesty, obedience and respect. Boys and girls were expected to be similar in their acquisition of these general characteristics. The practical skills to be developed and the chores assigned to each were different, however. Boys carried water and firewood, brought goods to market, learned to fish or produce feather crafts. Girls learned to spin and weave, cook, and were expected to be proficient at housework.

Formal education was compulsory for boys and girls, although girls generally attended for a shorter time. Beginning in early adolescence, formal teaching centered around songs, dances, and instrumental music. These were not only all essential to ritual and religious participation. Their content also transmitted important historical lessons and cultural values. By age fifteen, boys attended schools whose curricula included history, calendrics, dream interpretation, and the skills necessary for various occupations, such as hunter or priest. Military instruction formed the largest substance of commoner boys' formal education.

Law

The Aztec legal system incorporated both secular and supernatural sanctions in order to maintain social control. Behavior was expected to conform to established teachings. When it did not, threats of punishment were the items of first resort. Many religious traditions invoke banishment to "hell" or entry into "heaven" resulting as a consequence of an individual's conduct during life. Aztec belief, however, was that it was a person's death, and not their conduct in life, which determined events in the afterlife (Berdan 1982). Thus, no threat directed at an unpleasant afterlife could be issued.

Secular law was exacting and punishment was swift. Drunkenness was invoked as the cause of the vast majority of unacceptable public behavior and criminal activity. Adultery resulted in stoning or hanging; homicide was usually punishable by death, although in some cases the murderer was turned over to the victim's family to serve them in slavery. Stealing was less severely punished than any of the foregoing.

Pretending towards a higher social status than one's rightful one, either in the form of dress and personal adornment or acquisition of property, was punishable by death.

Supernatural sanctions were inflicted by the god responsible for punishing that offense, and the consequences would be ones which reflected the affront. Thus, the god Macuilxochitl would punish those who did not practice sexual abstinence during ritual fasts by inflicting venereal diseases. Other gods would retaliate if their shrines were not properly maintained, sending a variety of physical ailments which would identify the sufferer as one who had shirked some ritual responsibility.

POLITICAL ORGANIZATION

The Aztec empire boasted an intricately structured military and government. The type of political organization that predominated from the fourteenth through early sixteenth centuries was the city-state. Central Mexico was divided into some fifty or sixty of these units at this time, varying in size and political prowess.

Leadership and government

The degree of autonomy enjoyed by rulers (tlatoani) of the city-states was variable. Some were not beholden to any other authority, while others were dominated by leadership of a higher order, most typically rulers of Triple Alliance cities. (Berdan 1982)

The tlatoani functioned as a monarch. He was responsible for ritual, adjudication, waging war, and advocating for the rights of his citizens. In Tenochtitlan, the Mexica tlatoani was believed to be a descendent of the god Quetzalcoatl. Berdan (1982:100) reports: "The rulers were earthly counterparts of celestial deities; their rule was by divine right." While the position of tlatoani was an inherited one (often from brother to brother, and then to the first born son of the oldest brother), rulers had to have been

proven valorous in battle before ascending to leadership. In addition to his god-like status, he must possess great personal skills, especially in oratory.

The Council of Four, close relatives of the ruling tlatoani, chose his successor. Once selected, a series of rituals were set into motion, culminating in the coronation. First, the new tlatoani appeared before the priests, who escorted him (along with the Council) to a public ceremony, where citizens witnessed an offering of incense. The ruler and his council maintained a four day fast, after which they returned to the temple and cut themselves, offering blood to Huitzilopotchtli.

The custom after this initial offering was for the newly chosen tlataoni to leave for the battlefield and return with prisoners. At the coronation, to which rulers from both allied and enemy lands were invited, a spectacular feast was given, expensive gifts exchanged, and war prisoners captured by the new ruler were sacrificed. This display served to strengthen alliances and warn enemies. It also served as fair warning to any who would contemplate rebellion.

Tlatoani were assisted by special counselors, relatives with whom he consulted on all important governmental matters. Advice was given by specialists in each realm of the political structure. For military matters, he had a war council drawn from those professional warriors who had proven themselves in battle. Judicial advice was rendered by high court judges in the complex system of courts.

Warfare

Warfare has been called "a cultural preoccupation" (Berdan 1982) of the Mexica, woven into the fabric of social, political, economic, and religious life. Militaristic themes abound. A boy was declared a soldier at birth, and if his mother died in childbirth she was glorified as a warrior, and assured a blissful afterlife. Men were judged overwhelmingly by their militaristic skills, and rewarded commensurate with their valor. Victory in battle brought privileges in dress and ornamentation, as well as gifts. These returns were thought to inspire continued military success. Death in battle brought rewards in the afterlife.

If warfare was not quite itself a religion, it was at least bound up with religion. Not only did patron gods send them into battle, these same gods could only be appeased by human sacrifice gathered from enemy troops. There were even particular enemies whom the gods were thought to find especially pleasing. (Berdan 1982) War, far from being only a means to expand territory, functioned as an end in itself. The conquest of new lands was a pursuit separate from the warfare engendered by the need to capture people to be offered as sacrifice, and to provide militaristic experience for young soldiers. In fact, Aztecs staged ritual wars --known as "flower war," for the way in which men fell the ground like so many colorful blossoms shaken from a bough--expressly for the purpose of gathering prisoners to be sacrificed. (Townsend 1992)

Human sacrifice and cannibalism

While the topic of human sacrifice and cannibalism among the Aztec has generated much debate, there is no disagreement regarding the centrality of human sacrifice their culture. The practice arose out of a debt owed to the gods: the consequence of not paying was no less than the end of the world.

Aztec myth describes the creation of the sun and the moon, and the inception of their movement. When the current sun-- the fifth--was to be created, all the gods gathered at Teotihuacan to decide who would be willing to throw himself into a great fire and emerge as the sun. Two stepped forward, one wealthy and arrogant; the other poor and humble. As much as he wanted to be the sun, the arrogant god lacked the courage to throw himself into the flames Instead, the humble god cremated himself, and rose in the sky as the sun. Furious at being outdone, the first god followed, only to emerge as the moon, a pale reflection of the sun's great light. There they sat, together in the sky. The gods knew that they must be separated. One must shine brightly in the day, and the other glow at night. One god threw a rabbit at the moon, some say to dim its light, others say to keep it distant from the sun. Even when this was done, the sun and moon still hung, unmoving, in the sky. It was then that the gods sacrificed themselves, for only their blood could put the sun in motion. Life for humankind was only possible with a moving sun, and this the gods provided. It then became the responsibility of humanity to feed the sun thereafter, lest it stop, and the universe cease with it. Although mythology states that sacrifice is to the sun, the wider notion is that there can be no human life without sacrificial human death. (Berdan 1982)

The most common form of sacrifice was to open a man's chest with a sacred blade, tear out the still-beating heart, and offer it to the gods. Women occasionally had their heads severed before their hearts were removed. Children were most often drowned, securing good rainfall. (Berdan 1982)

Special occasions and ceremonies dictated variations in the form of sacrifice, although the removal of the heart and display of the head were consistent. Priests upon occasion ceremonially wore the skin of a flayed victim. All forms of sacrifice were sacred, performed without vengeance and endured without regret. A captor honored and respected the person to be sacrificed. Those who died in this fashion were privileged to be the food of the gods. In dying to keep the world alive, they were assured a sublime afterlife.

Often, once the sacrifice was completed, the body was stewed and ritually consumed. Ritual cannibalism has been explained by some anthropologists as a religious phenomenon, while others propose an ecological explanation.

Those who see cannibalism as an extension of the religious motivation behind human sacrifice, suggest that sacrifice made the victims divine. Eating the divine then made the consumer sacred.

Thus, the belief that sacrifice is demanded by the gods and necessary for survival makes eating the flesh of the sacrificial victim an extension of the ritual process of maintaining the universe.

Those who argue against such a supernatural stance suggest that there were nutritional reasons for the practice of cannibalism, chief among them, the deficiency of protein and fat in the Aztec diet. Formulated by anthropologist Michael Harner (1977), this theory proposes that cannibalism may have been couched in religious explanations, but in fact this practice alleviated a severe need for protein. If there was indeed a shortage of protein, feeding captives would only exacerbate the problem: sacrifice obviated the need to provision a prisoner, and cannibalism provided protein.

This assertion has been severely challenged on many grounds, including the fact that those who might be in greatest need of protein (commoners, children and adolescents) were least likely to receive human flesh, accessible most typically to nobles. Moreover, there is debate as to whether protein deficiency existed in the first place. (Berdan 1982)

Population control is another motivation proposed for cannibalism, although this aim could hardly be best served by the sacrifice of adult males (the most usual offerings) rather than women of childbearing age. (Berdan 1982)

RELIGION AND EXPRESSIVE CULTURE

The Aztec world view maintained that life was precarious, and it was the responsibility of humankind to attempt to control this uncertainty and assure their own continued existence.

Every half century, a dramatic ritual was undertaken. All fires were extinguished, all houses swept clean, all hearthstones and cooking pots were discarded. The entire population was awakened at night; babies, if they slept, would be turned into mice. They waited, poised, to hear of success in the ritual about to begin. Priests climbed to the top of a mountain in the dark, and sacrificed a victim, attempting to kindle a fire in his open chest cavity. If the spark caught, life would continue for another half century. Citizens were notified of the new fire, and as they waited for messengers to bring them flames to start their own fires, they cut their ears and offered blood to the gods upon hearing the news. Should the fire not start, the sun would grow cold, and the universe end. This ritual embodied the most salient tenets of Aztec culture: that the continuation of life is not assured unless the people actively promote its survival through human sacrifice.

Aztec gods

Aztec deities functioned in many ways like patron saints. Most were envisioned anthropomorphically, with human traits. Each calpulli had its own deity, and because, as we have seen, calpullis were often groups of occupational specialists, these deities came to be associated with the occupational group.

When the Mexica arrived in the Valley of Mexico, they found numerous cults which had grown up around gods of nature and which the Aztec made their own. Berdan (1982) describes theirs as an assimilative religion, rather than a proselytizing one. They embraced the deities of those they conquered, and soon had a myriad of gods. Townsend (1992) suggests that the conquest of each enemy town might be viewed as the "capture" of their deity.

These have been roughly divided into three categories: gods believed responsible for creation, those associated with the elements, and those who are affiliated with war--and thus sacrifice.

The creation deities are ones which might best be described as supreme--they are the high gods, more abstract and omnipotent. Included among these are gods of fire, which is an important Aztec theme.

Priests devoted most of their rituals to the gods associated with rain, human fertility, and agricultural fecundity. These gods controlled the elements, on which the survival of the people depended. The majority of female gods, responsible for both subsistence and birth, are found in this pantheon of deities of the elements.

Huitzilopotchli, the patron deity of the Mexica who guided their journey into the valley, is a sun god categorized with the sacrificial war gods. The tie between warriors and the sun was direct and critical: it was only through the blood of sacrifice that the sun could be fed, and kept alive. And it was largely through military capture that the staggering number of victims required could be supplied.

Aztec priests

Because each of the numerous gods claimed their own temples, were honored by their own rituals, and made their own particularistic demands, each needed a host of priests to serve its needs.

The structure of the priesthood closely resembled the structure of the rest of Aztec society, in its hierarchical, "pyramidal" nature. (Townsend 1992) It was from among the nobility that the most powerful priests were drawn, although even the lowest ranking commoner had access to the priestly role.

Both women and men served in the priesthood, and infant girls and boys were often dedicated by their parents at birth. (Fewer women than men remained in the priesthood for the duration of their lifetime, however.)

The majority of a priest's duties revolved around service to their deity. The idol must be cared for, its surroundings clean, temple fires lighted, and prayers and penance were offered day and night. Priests were expected to regularly offer up their own blood, and the display of their penance smeared on their temple was an important sign of their dedication. A secondary duty of the priesthood was interpreting sacred texts and educating boys of the nobility. Priests used meditation, fasting, purifying baths, and occasionally hallucinogenic drugs as means to more effectively serve their deity.

Rites and ceremonies

Aztec rituals and ceremonies were very much tied up with their reckoning of time. They kept an annual ceremonial calendar based on the 365 day solar year; but also reckoned time by a 260 day ritual calendar. (This calendar contains the "moveable feasts," which are any religious festivals unfixed to the solar calendar, such that they may fall on a different date each year. [Berdan 1982]) The 260 and 365 day calendars have been conceptualized as two gears fitted side by side: when turning, the first days would align every fifty-two years. It is this alignment that gives rise to the half century fire-lighting ceremony mentioned above. (Townsend 1992)

Ceremonies occurred with great frequency: there were eighteen regularly scheduled rituals each month. The vast majority of these had to do with petitioning the gods associated with fertility, rain, and agriculture. Many of these included fasting, and offerings of some sort--from incense to human sacrifice--were always a part of every ceremony.

Magic and omens

The formal religious system, with its elaborate rituals and supplication to powerful deities, existed alongside a more intimate and personal system of divination and magic. Shamans acted not on behalf of a deity worshipped by the masses, but for an individual petitioner who wished to manipulate the directives of the supernatural world.

Diviners played an important role in a belief system that saw an individual's fate as being predetermined. Although ones destiny was to a large extent fixed, it could be manipulated to some degree by following the recommendations of a diviner hired to "read" an infant's fate, and suggest which days might afford the child the best its destiny could offer.

Divination was relied upon most heavily for prediction, but could also be propitious in healing. To this end, shamans ingested hallucinogens to grant them access to divine information. They were able to read signs of illness by throwing grains of maize on a piece of cloth and interpreting their pattern, predict recovery by whether a knotted rope held fast or gave way, determine the severity of soul loss by the clarity of a child's reflection in a mirror.

Those illness with supernatural causes required supernatural intercession to effect a cure, and a shaman would be called upon to intervene.

Since they were ruled by fate, and their destiny was already planned, it was only to be expected that Aztecs must look around them for omens informing them of their destiny. Some omens were to be found in the behavior of birds and animals; others might be supernatural materializations.

Aztec arts and sciences

The arts and sciences of the Aztecs were a blend of the scientific and the symbolic. This body of knowledge included calendars that were based on rigorous astronomical calculations, but were used for ritual purposes. The practice of medicine employed a chemically-active pharmacopoeia, but these agents were always used along with shamanistic divination. Complex technologies produced crafts that were used in religious ceremonies. (Berdan 1982)

Aztec writing was hieroglyphic, which demanded great skill in memorization, since the glyphs could only serve to jog the memory when looking through a text already known to the reader. Such skills were possessed solely by the nobility, who were the only literate members of Aztec society. The most common form of hieroglyphic was the pictograph, a stylized drawing of the object. Glyphs could also be ideographic, using one aspect of an object to represent the entire object itself. For example, a scroll to represent a speech

to be given, footprints to represent a journey, or arrows and a shield to represent war. A third form of hieroglyphics was a phonetic system in which a word for which there was an easily-drawn picture was used to represent a more abstract word which sounded the same. (This is a device commonly employed in "rebus" puzzles, where a sheep (ewe) might be drawn to stand for the word "you.")

Stone sculpture of human and animal figures was a skill which was formally taught, and that led to a style of stoneworking that is readily recognizable. Craftwork in mosaics, gold, and feathers was also highly standardized; taught within the guilds, consistency of style is found within each medium.

Literature and music were highly valued, as were oratory skills. While speech-making skills were generally only taught in noble schools, songs and dances were part of all mandatory education. Since a large number of people spanning all the social classes participated in the numerous religious rituals, it was imperative that all citizens be trained in these skills.

CONQUEST

For ten years prior to Spanish conquest, the Mexica had been visited by portentous omens. These were difficult to interpret specifically, but rulers were certain they foretold Aztec doom.

Finally, messengers reported sighting strangers off the coast. This was the final and most frightening omen. One year later, these strangers were back, led by Hernán Cortés. In 1519, Cortés and several hundred soldiers began to advance on Tenochtitlan. As they neared the Aztec city, they heard stories about the riches contained within, and pressed on, determined. When Cortés reached the city he captured the Mexica ruler, and violent battles ensued. The siege on the Aztec city lasted more than seventy days, with tens of thousands killed. Despite their valiant defense, the Aztecs were overcome.

AZTEC

Although the Spaniards were smaller in number, their technology and strategies afforded them a great advantage. Their militaristic training taught them to fight to kill, not to capture. They had swords and muskets, horses and large dogs.

One of the first consequences of Spanish conquest was the decimation of the native population. By the early seventeenth century a population of fifteen million had been reduced to just one million. Not only warfare, but introduced diseases, famine, overwork under Spanish rule, and displacement all took their toll.

Within ten years of the fall of Tenochtitlan, most of Mesoamerica was under Spanish rule. As more Spaniards arrived, the surrounding culture was changed. To the agricultural system were added Spanish technologies: the wheeled cart pulled by draft animals, machetes, plows. The introduction of both livestock and new crops contributed to the decline in the indigenous population by usurping much of the land formerly devoted to maize (Berdan 1982).

Aztec society became less stratified under Spanish rule. As is commonly the case under colonial rule, ascribed statuses gave way to achieved ones. Spaniards, not Aztecs, held the high political offices. Friars converted indigenous peoples to Christianity. Worship of Aztec deities was forbidden, along with its rituals of human sacrifice. Some indigenous peoples found ways to blend many of the similarities of the two systems of belief. Both Christianity and the Aztec religion contained rites of baptism and confession, and a belief in virgin birth. The multitude of Aztec deities became linked with the many Catholic saints.

The Mexica had been conquered. Aztec and Spanish cultures combined over the ensuing hundreds of years to produce an amalgam, a new way of life.

REFERENCES

BERDAN, F.
1982   *The Aztecs of Central Mexico: An Imperial Society.* New York: Holt, Rinehart & Winston.

HARNER, M.
1977   The Ecological Basis for Aztec Sacrifice. *American Ethnologist* 4:117-135.

LEON-PORTILLA, M.
1992   *The Aztec Image of Self and Society.* Salt Lake City: University of Utah Press.

TOWNSEND, R.F.
1992   *The Aztecs.* London: Thames and Hudson, Ltd.

§ THE BEGINNING

The Basseri have always been. We have always been on this land; we were created from its dust.

INTRODUCTION AND ECOLOGY

The Basseri are a pastoral nomadic society in southern Iran, who migration takes them to the mountains and steppes to the east, north, and south.

The land in which they travel spans about three hundred miles in length, and about fifty miles in width. They are never too greatly dispersed as they journey.

The province in which the Basseri live is quite ethnically heterogeneous, and it has been suggested (Barth 1964) that the tribes in the area are better distinguished from one another on the basis of political organization than by any ethnic or geographic boundaries. Using this criterion, the Basseri do form a discrete unit, operating under the governance of one chief, and they are recognized as such by the Iranian government.

Numbering about 16,000 individuals (or three thousand tents), the Basseri are associated with other groups in the area who either claim origins within the Basseri, or common heritage with them. The tribe's nomadic lifestyle was interrupted for a time, when the reign of Reza Shah dictated enforced settlement. During this period only a small number of Basseri continued their nomadic ways. Many more remained sedentary, to the detriment of their flocks and people. Once Reza Shah's reign was concluded fifty years ago, the Basseri were able to resume their traditional life, and most did so.

Basseri territory is diverse, ranging from desert to mountain. Throughout their range there is little rain, this is concentrated in the winter months. Precipitation in the mountains falls as snow, and thus there is more vegetation and forested land in the mountainous areas. Where the land is flat and low, drought defines the summer and there is very little vegetation, limited to a thin cover of grass during winter rains and into the early spring.

For those sedentary people surrounding the Basseri, agriculture provides the main pattern of subsistence, dependent almost entirely upon irrigation. Rivers and streams in the area provide water for irrigation, and horses and oxen are also employed to pull water up from wells. Access to groundwater is gained by a series of underground aqueducts which link groups of wells, funneling groundwater from higher elevations down to the valley lowlands.

The pastures upon which the Basseri pastoral economy depends are seasonal, necessitating that they have access to an extensive amount of pasture area. The land through which they move affords them this diversity. In the winter, the northern areas are covered with snow, but the south still has usable pasture land. In the spring, areas of low and middle altitude have plentiful grazing areas. As they start to dry out, there are better areas at higher elevations. Although Fall is the most tenuous time, once fields are harvested agriculturalists are pleased to have nomads graze their flocks on the land, since the manure acts as excellent fertilizer.

The Basseri, like other major nomadic tribes, have a traditional migratory route which they follow annually. In addition to specifying which lands they use, this schedule also elaborates when they will arrive at each location, and the duration of their stay. This route and the schedule of utilization along the way is the il-rah, the "tribal road," and each il-rah is considered the property of that tribe. It grants them rights to particular land at a specific time, and is recognized by the peoples with whom they come in contact. It is important to note that it is not only access to lands, but access at a specific time, that is granted: many tribes use the same land, as the il-rah doesn't give exclusive utilization rights. But the lands are validly used only at particular times; thus, tribes who "share" the same land do not overlap in their time there.

The group does not always stay together. As they move north, alternative routes within the il-rah allow some dispersal of the tribe, some of whom stay longer in the more abundant spring fields,

others choosing to foray east to villages recently made accessible to them.

Breaking camp and moving on is usually a daily activity, but in the summertime the Basseri tend to become more stationary, with movement only local during the day, returning to the same encampment at night. The return journey begins in the late summer and early fall, and usually includes stops to earn cash for labor: otherwise stops are few on this leg of the trek. Fields have the least to offer in this season. Winter too is a more stationery time, when local forays predominate.

ECONOMIC ORGANIZATION

Subsistence and manufacture

Domesticated animals are of paramount importance to the Basseri. Sheep and goats are the most important, because it is they who provide the bulk of subsistence products. Donkeys are used as pack animals, and are ridden by women and children. Men ride horses, which carry no other load. Camels are burdened with the heaviest items to transport. The Basseri herd no cattle because their trek is long and difficult, and the terrain is too rocky for cattle to navigate. (Barth 1964)

Just as different cultigens are suited to particular environments, so too are strains of domesticated animals. There are several varieties of sheep in this area, and the nomadic strain is particularly well-suited for the migratory life of the Basseri. These sheep are ill-suited to the extremes of temperature found in the north and south. While those raised in the north have an increased tolerance for the cold, and those domesticated in the south are better able to withstand drought and dry grazing land, the sheep kept by the Basseri fare best in moderate climate. Thus, the tribes movement not only insures access to grazing, it preserves the health of the herds they graze. (Reportedly, nomads who settle in either northern or southern regions and attempt to raise the same strain of sheep with which they are accustomed to migrate lose nearly eighty percent of their animals. [Barth 1964])

Each shepherd is generally responsible for a mixed flock of three or four hundred sheep and goats. Young animals are kept away from older ones, and milk is preserved for human consumption by preventing over-nursing of lambs and kids.

Each individual household must own about one hundred sheep and goats in order to provide for itself satisfactorily. Although the average household falls somewhat short of this ideal, the Basseri are known to be possessed of a relatively high standard of living when compared to other populations in their area. (Barth 1964)

Milk and milk products are the staples of the Basseri diet. Sheeps' and goats' milk, mixed together, are never consumed without being heated. When a bit of sour milk (or the acidic contents of a lamb's stomach) are added, the fresh milk sours. Cheese, which is then made from junket, a sour milk product, is not produced during the times of daily tribal movement. Such production is usually reserved for the more sedentary summer encampment periods.

Sour milk is also stored, by separating the curds from the whey. The solid curds are shaped into dumpling-like balls, dried in the sun, and are preserved in that fashion through the winter months. The liquid whey can be fed to the watchdogs. When sour milk is churned into buttermilk or butter, it can provide income; while buttermilk is usually immediately consumed, and butter largely eaten fresh, quantities of butter are also stored for sale.

Beyond those numbers of young animals needed to supplement the adult herd, lambs and kids (usually male) are slaughtered for meat, and their hides sold. Lambskin is a much-sought product at market, and it is hides that provide all the containers for storage and transport.

In addition to milk products and hides, the animals also provide wool both for sale and for the tribe's own use. Wool may be spun and woven, or processed into rope.

Such spinning and weaving requires great skill and consumes the majority of Basseri women's leisure time. Using threads they have themselves spun, women fashion all the saddlebags and cloth packs in which are carried the entire inventory of the tribe's belongings. Carpets and rugs for sleeping are similarly crafted. Their tents are made of woven goat hair, which renders them impermeable to rain, and insulated such that heat is retained in the cooler months and dissipated in the summertime.

Foraging plays a role of minor importance in the subsistence strategies of the Basseri. Hunting of large game is sport; springtime brings the collection of a few plants and wild mushrooms.

The Basseri milk-based diet is importantly supplemented by cereals and grains, the production of which is a relatively recent phenomenon. During the more settled summer months, wheat and other cereals can be planted upon arrival, and will be matured for harvesting before the time camp is broken. Often, they will contract with settled local residents to plant crops before they themselves arrive to do the harvesting. This agricultural work is neither enjoyed nor highly valued: many nomads refuse to participate at all and look down upon those who do (Barth 1964). Some Basseri are landowners, and although they do not settle on the land they own, such possession allows them to avoid all agricultural work by leasing the land to others in return for a portion of the yield.

Given their nomadic lifestyle, many of the tribes necessities must be secured by trade. The most important of these is flour: unleavened bread is part of every meal. Sugar, tea, fruits and vegetables are similarly obtained. Basseri bring to market butter, wool and hides, and occasionally animals. For these they are able to obtain clothing, cooking utensils, saddles, and luxury items--which may include such diverse products as jewelry, narcotics and portable radios. (Barth 1964)

BASSERI

Residence patterns

Each independent Basseri household is a nuclear family living in a single tent. These constitute the basic unit of production and consumption, and ownership of livestock.

Large tents are pitched for longer stays; for daily travel, smaller versions are employed. Camps are generally made up of thirty or forty tents, occupied by a married couple and their children, with an occasional widowed or single relative.

Although some goods may be owned by particular family members, it is the household which is regarded as the property owning unit. Within the household unit, there is a very clear division of labor and vesting of authority. The household is represented in tribal matters and dealings with outsiders by the head, who is invariably male. If the tent consists of a nuclear family, the husband/father is the head. If not, the senior male assumes this role. If there is no adult male residing within the household, a woman may be regarded as the head, but she will actually be represented by a male relative in formal matters.

Within the domestic domain, however, there is much more egalitarianism. Decisions concerning family, children, marriage, kinship, as well as the wider realm of social and group relations are made by adults in consultation with one another. The household's most assertive or wisest member will predominate, regardless of gender. (Barth 1964)

Most food preparation, sewing, and washing are by and large girls' and womens' chores. Boys and men haul water and wood (although not exclusively so), roast meat and make tea, and some wash their own clothes.

The Basseri will strike camp and move an average of one day out of every three. This pattern of such frequent movement demands great organization and physical labor. A day when the tribe is planning to move starts long before sunrise. The herds will depart first, under the guidance of a girl, boy, or man. The tent will be down before it is light, and the donkeys are rounded up to be loaded with possessions. The leader of the egress will be a man of the tribe who owns a horse, and rides ahead. The average daily trek is about three hours (at a fast pace) before the tents are repitched. The shepherded animals arrive after the people, since they cannot travel at the same brisk pace as the caravan of families on donkeys. Once the animals have been milked, a meal can be prepared. At sunset the animals are milked again, and the late meal is eaten before sleep.

Milking is made most efficient by herding the animals into a triangular formation, with the animals at the apex driven past individuals who remain in place filling buckets as the animals are milked and then allowed to wander off. This allows the milkers (a role filled by both men and women) to stay put, and assures that each animal has been milked.

SOCIAL ORGANIZATION

New and cooperative households

As is typically found in groups whose households are based on nuclear families, the Basseri are also neolocal; that is, upon marriage a couple starts their own nuclear family in a new tent.

Initially upon marriage, a woman will join her husband in his family's tent, but this is only a temporary arrangement. As soon as they can, a new couple will establish themselves as an independent unit. In order to accomplish this, however, they must be able to support themselves.

Since individual family members may own property, it is common for fathers to give several animals to their sons in times of plenty when the family can afford to do so. This practice, in part, teaches the boy how to care for the animals, which can later be taken to his own household upon his marriage. Boys may also work as shepherds for other households, and receive payment in lambs. A diligent worker may be able to build up a small herd of his own.

In addition, the groom's father will pay a cash bride price to the bride's father; some of this, it is expected, will be used to purchase goods the new couple will need for their own tent--rugs, blankets, cooking utensils. Women of both families weave the cloth to be used by the new couple to construct their tent.

While all of this helps launch the bride and groom on their way, it does not provide the couple with the size flock necessary for their survival and success. This deficiency is overcome by the practice called "anticipatory inheritance:" that is, a son receives upon his marriage that portion of his father's flock to which he would be rightful heir at his father's death. (Barth 1964) (When a man actually dies, the additional animals he has amassed, as well as those he originally retained for himself, are also inherited, once his surviving spouse has received her due.)

Once the new couple has been settled in their household and is in possession of their flock, they are faced with the challenge of performing the whole range of tasks associated with the nomadic lifestyle, and this is not possible with a household consisting of only a husband and wife. The ideal configuration has, at minimum, an adult male who performs the labor associated with his role and takes his place in the leadership portion of the migration, an adult female who accomplishes the numerous and difficult domestic tasks, and at least one individual who acts as shepherd. The nuclear family unit can certainly eventually attain this form, but there are long periods of time both before there are children of shepherding age and after the children have grown and are on their own. For these portions of the household's life cycle, the additional labor necessary must be contracted for in some fashion. A shepherd may be hired or a close relative adopted, but more often families band together to form small cooperative units which shared herding tasks.

Both the strategies of hiring a shepherd or adopting a child allow an individual household to remain an independent unit by relying on labor from outside sources. As Barth (1964:21) points out, "This independence and self-sufficiency of the nomad household, whereby it can survive in economic relation with an external market but in complete isolation from all fellow nomads, is a very striking and fundamental feature of Basseri organization."

However, in tandem with this independence, several households usually combine their flocks under the care of one shepherd. It is not difficult for a single shepherd to control up to four hundred animals; with cooperation among the adults at milking time (who milk their own household's animals), this system is quite efficient.

Those families who have entered into such an arrangement generally pitch their tents together at night, and regard each other as equal partners. A family may feel free to cease its participation in this cooperative at any time, and as families shift alliances the clusters of households change over time. Often these shifts in composition are the result either of disagreements or the assessment of the skills of one's current partners relative to the skills of others whom one might join. Since there only has to be one individual in all the joined households who can serve as shepherd, the usual pattern is for smaller or newer households to join more stable or populous ones.

Camps

During the spring when fodder in pastures is plentiful, nomadic tribes can be supported in large numbers. During the winter months, however, it is greatly to their advantage to set up camp in smaller groups. Although each section of land holds little in the way of resources, the total amount of land is extensive. By dispersing over a wide range, they can best use the depleted environment. Thus, while at other times of year Basseri camps may have as many as forty tents, during the winter local camps generally are made up of just a handful.

Barth (1964) has noted that in many ways these camps resemble the small village of sedentary groups. Whatever sense of community is found among the Basseri is contained in the local encampments they set up along their migratory route, and the members of each camp constitute a "clearly bounded social group." (p. 25) It is only with one another that they have consistent and continuous relationships; all their other contacts are fleeting.

Maintaining this sense of community is a unique challenge among nomadic peoples, as it is unlike that which is found in a sedentary population. For settled peoples, life as a community persists unless some active change is made. Each day the alliances between people are reinforced by the usual progression of the daily routine. Should dissolution of any part of the community be anticipated, it would require that households disband and individuals take dramatic action. For tribes with a nomadic lifestyle, however, the decision to remain a community is not a passive one, dependent upon the inertia of routine. Each day, residents of a local camp must convene and assess their surroundings in order to make the crucial decision of whether or not to move on, and if so, how far. This is not a choice to be made whimsically; the health of their herds and the economic base of their existence is at stake. The wisdom of each individual household head will decide his family's fate, and there must be agreement among tents in order to proceed. While arguments and differences of opinion between villagers may be resolved after some "cooling off" period--sedentary peoples are unlikely to abandon their homes permanently as a result of a single disputed decision--once nomadic households fail to reach consensus about daily migration, they have effectively changed the composition of their community. As Barth (1964:26) puts it: "by next evening they will be separated by perhaps 20 km of open steppe and by numerous other camps, and it will have become quite

complicated to arrange for a reunion. The maintenance of a camp as a social unit thus requires the daily unanimous agreement by all members on economically vital questions."

Reaching consensus about daily movement is greatly facilitated by the recognition of a single leader in each camp. This individual both represents his own local group in dealings with other camps, and influences the decision-making within his own.

The Basseri, as will be discussed later, are united as a tribe under the authority of a single chief. The chief appoints local headmen who are recognized as having been so chosen, but are not endowed with any formal means to enforce their own will. There are fewer officially appointed headmen, however, than there are local camps in need of leadership. In those camps where no headman is in residence, informal leaders take the helm. These individual local leaders, however, are not his representatives of the chief, and cannot invoke his wishes or support in their own edicts.

The status of headman is typically an inherited one, and usually passes from a man to his next most senior relative. However, camp members claim as their right the ability to bypass such rules and select the person whom they see as most deserving of the position. (And, in addition, the right to unseat a headman they deem unfit.) The chief is expected to acquiesce in this regard, and generally does so: it is certainly in his best interest to have as his representative the individual most likely to succeed in leading his own group. The chief can then rely on the status and authority already established by a local leader to add weight to his own.

The requirements for acceding to the position of headman is in part dependent upon his economic position within the group, but this is minimal and somewhat tenuous. Wealth is, by and large, livestock. And all Basseri are subject to the loss of animals through circumstances out of their control. Thus, wealth is not a station upon which anyone can depend. (It is reported that in some cases of serious animal loss suffered by headmen, group members decide to maintain his position by donating their own animals to reform his herd. [Barth 1964]). Moreover, even though prestige is gained through ownership of a large herd, it does not appear that wealth is easily converted into political authority.

Since a headman's power is entirely contained within the confines of his own camp, the range of his authority is limited. Barth (1964) reminds us of the structure of Basseri society: each tent is very much an autonomous unit; herding units of two to five tents come together for economic reasons and in so doing form an economic unit which is self-sufficient; the headman receives no specific empowerment by the chief. Therefore, the power base of the headman is very narrow indeed, and often restricted to his own unit. This is, as Barth (1964:29) remarks, "a very small base from which to attempt to tyrannize a whole camp."

Kinship

The Basseri, like other tribal groups in the Middle East, reckon descent patrilineally. Inheritance is usually from father to son, and other patrikin will supplant daughters in obtaining land rights and other goods. A son of a Basseri is a Basseri, regardless of the affiliation of his mother: a woman bestows no membership rights to her own tribe on her offspring. There is a particularly strong solidarity among brothers, and the relationship of a man to his father, father's brothers, and grandfather is one of great deference and respect. Local groups are often formed by brothers, who have had joint rights to their father's flock before their own marriages and choose to remain associated after their inheritance of animals upon marriage.

While patrilineal kinship is a driving force behind group formation (and access to headman status), there is a strong tie between some matrikin. The relationship between a child and mother's brother is a particularly affectionate and indulgent one.

Marriage

Alliances between households are most often reinforced by affinal (marital) ties. Marriages are arranged by household heads, which are usually the fathers of the prospective bride and groom. In his absence, a brother or father's brother will serve. Thus, except in the case of an adult man who is arranging his own subsequent marriage, a marital contract is not primarily a bond between a bride and groom, but is rather a transaction between tents. (In fact, the typical term of reference by a man to his daughter-in-law is "my bride." [Barth 1964])

Bride price among the Basseri is called "milk-price," which pays for both the woman's hand in marriage as well as the household items she will bring along with her. There is also an "insurance" fee promised, which will be the woman's compensation should the marriage end in divorce. Before the wedding takes place, there are minor tokens given to the bride and her family by the prospective groom, as well as some small acts of bride service (in the form of small favors) to her parents.

Although there are no ongoing debts or obligations between the families once the marriage has taken place, there appears to be great affection engendered between the households of children who marry one another. The woman no longer has a formal affiliation with her parents' household, but since her in-laws and parents will work to actively maintain a friendship, she remains "connected." These warm ties between households are sought in future marriages: sister exchange (where a groom's sister is given to the bride's family in compensation for the bride) is common, and the Basseri conform to the rules of the levirate and sororate (replacing a deceased spouse with an analagous family member), even in the face of protest by the individuals involved. Families also seek to perpetuate these ties in subsequent generations of marriage arrangements.

Barth (1964) suggests that this extreme affection and active pursuit of the continuation of affinal ties may derive from the political and economic independence of the Basseri nuclear family unit. The only way to insure the continuation of the community of these autonomous units is to knit households together by marriage. This is especially salient in light of the "anticipatory inheritance" of herds upon marriage. Siblings each receive their portion of their father's livestock and establish their own separate household while he is alive. There is no further bond between them save that of affection; no further inheritance of any substantial nature remains to link them economically. (Since women retain no rights in their family of origin, this is equally true for female siblings.) Marital ties, especially if they involve siblings marrying into the same family, can serve to keep tents allied with one another, thus preserving the nomadic community.

A Basseri woman is very important economically; there is a high level of mutual dependence between husband and wife, and women possess tremendous authority within the domestic sphere, which in migratory peoples is the one unchanging portion of their environment. The household cannot survive without a woman's labor. Her family remains important to her both emotionally and also, to some extent, socially, in that they retain influence over her future marriage should she be widowed (or divorced, though this is rare). A husband wishes to maintain friendly relations with his in-laws in part to assure his good relationship with his wife, who is economically crucial to the household.

The desire to maintain ties that will generate good will in a local camp, and thus foster consensus in daily migratory decisions and solidarity in general, results in a high number of marriages between close kin. The camp is an endogamous group; when Basseri speak of their camp to outsiders, they refer to it as if it were a single lineage. Barth points out that the truly bilateral camp structure works against the formation of patrilineages. Within each tent, husband and wife are virtual equals; in external dealings, however, the husband is the undisputed head of the household.

So it is that while externally giving the impression of revolving around a patrilineal core, the camp is composed, in fact, of "bilateral, nearly self-perpetuating kin groups." (1964:41)

Distance as "social idiom"

The actual distance maintained between tents in a Basseri camp can be an indicator of social distance between their occupants. If dissension occurs at the end of a day's journey, participants in the argument will pitch their tents at opposite ends of the campsite. Resolution of differences will be indicated by the tents eventually being pitched in closer proximity in subsequent encampments.

There are practical considerations too in the placement of tents. Households that cooperate in herding must pitch their tents near one another in order to be near their comingled animals. (And, following from this, these units might maintain some distance from other households cooperating together, to avoid mixing corporate herds.) In addition, camp configuration may be determined by the environment: often the shape of the camping site itself will dictate the placement of tents, since with each stop the tribe is presented with a site of potentially different dimensions than the last.

This lack of persistent cohesive groups within the tribe (beyond that of the herding unit) is demonstrated not only when the group is encamped, but also as they migrate. Although the morning ritual of breaking camp usually occurs at the same time for all households, individual families leave whenever their tent is down and their belongings are packed. The group does not wait until everyone is ready before the commence the trek. Smaller families and those with fewer belongings to pack may routinely set out first, with the last family departing half and hour later. This results in the scattering of a group over at least a mile's length, moving at varying paces. The herds move slowest, stopping to graze along the way. The caravan of donkeys and camels who carry the packed belongings stay on the main route and travel at a faster pace. Men on horseback ride on ahead, and are the ones to reach the stopping point first; it is they who choose the campsite.

There are three decisions which face the Basseri daily: whether or not to move on a particular day, which route to follow, and where to make the new camp. The first decision especially demands unanimity, since the routes are limited and the new camp is chosen by the front riders. Each day the leader must attempt to have all heads of households decide to stay on-site another day, or move on. Barth found it quite striking that despite the critical nature of this decision and the necessity for agreement in its resolution, there was a complete lack of any group assemblage to come to a decision. There was such circuitous discussion that often the residents went to sleep at night not knowing whether they would be moving on in the morning.

He explains this phenomenon by invoking the character of the influence possessed by the tribal leaders. The leader's voice is not given much more weight than anyone else's, in an absolute sense. His strategy, then, is to gather together singly or in small groups those people over whom he has sway owing to ties of friendship or kinship. These people can then form a larger group of singular opinion to talk with others, and these become more and more numerous until there is a clear majority opinion. This majority view is so important that often people endeavor to qualify what they say in such a way that it takes a trained listener to know which side the speaker is advocating; he will always present both sides, so as not to end up siding with the minority. This leads to conversation which often seems pointless. (Barth (1964:45) recalls, "Not only does the frustrated anthropologist remain in the dark [as to] whether he will have to pack his stuff and move on next morning; he cannot even learn about herding and nomadic life from these hour-long discussions, when points which are bandied about and emphasized by all, turn out to be without substantive relevance to the problem.")

Association with individuals outside of local camp members is infrequent; even contact with other Basseri is rare. This intense isolation results in part from the great feelings of suspicion borne by the group: no one ventures outside the circle of tents at night. Theirs is a world which is warm and comfortable within the confines of the cluster of tents. Beyond this world lies a world of strangers who are likely robbers and thieves. (Barth 1964) Since this is a feeling shared with other local groups, there is rarely any hostility between camps--everyone is more than willing to keep their distance.

POLITICAL ORGANIZATION

The Basseri encampment's isolation and autonomy is a core feature of life for the members of each local group. Some camps have many tents and some have few; some trace their ancestry such that they claim origins from, or memberships in, larger groupings. They consider themself--and are considered by others-- to be one unified tribe because they are all subsumed under the authority of a single leader, the chief of all Basseri.

Chieftainship

The position of chief among the Basseri is typical of Middle Eastern centralized leadership, in that it is thought that power emanates from him, rather than having been vested in him by those he leads (Barth 1964).

The chief and his close kin are set apart from all other Basseri in several ways. First, they are seen as descended from a noble lineage, and part of the respect shown them, and the authority granted them, derive from this distinction. Furthermore, they are quite removed from the nomadic life: they own land and houses, villages, and herds numbering in the thousands.

The chief is expected to conduct himself in a manner befitting a man of power and privilege. He is expected to live lavishly and bestow gifts generously. In order to accomplish this, he must depend on more than inheritence to supply his wealth, and he does. Taxes, payable in sheep, are imposed on the tribe members, resulting in the collection of nearly eight thousand sheep a year. (Annual taxes of butter are also paid, and gifts are expected to be brought to the chief by anyone who comes before him.)

In the realm of decision-making, the chief's behavior is clearly unique. The typical Basseri style of collective judgments, subtle persuasion, and reaching consensus is not in evidence when chiefly decisions are made. He retains the sole prerogative to command, and to render decisions which affect an individual living in another tent. (Barth (1964) recalls that he was reminded of the chief's monopoly on the right to dictate when he himself made a suggestion regarding the movement of the camp in which he lived, asserting that he would take responsibility for the consequences; he was reprimanded for acting like a chief and attempting to usurp rights that were the chief's alone.)

The headmen appointed by the chief are his representatives but do not act in his stead. They function most often as relayers of information and not as enforcers of his will; thus they are links in the chain of communication, but not in a chain of command (Barth 1964).

The chief's responsibilities revolve around allotting pastures and the organizing of migratory patterns, settling disputes, and acting as the tribe's representative with outside authorities.

The development of patterns of travel and use of grazing land among a large population is a monumental feat. It involves coordinating a regular schedule which eliminates both overuse of land and a logjam of peoples moving along a particular road. This falls to the chief and his administrator, and without this tightly orchestrated direction, a nomadic lifestyle would be unworkable. (Salzman 1974). Among other nomadic peoples in Iran,,

allotment of pastures is often used as a method of sanction, and it has been suggested that this practice exists among the Basseri as well (Salzman 1974). Chiefs among other tribes will limit access to some lands and condemn individuals to the use of lesser pastures as a form of punishment.

The chief's role as adjudicator of disputes is one which is relied upon only after the customary strategies of discussion and compromise at the camp level have been exhausted. Those cases that prove impossible to settle (or involve people with whom it appears "impossible" to reason) are brought before the chief and those involved must abide by his decision.

The Basseri are part of a plural society, and as such the chief's role as their representative to both the Iranian government as well as non-Basseri peoples is crucial. The importance of this function in a plural society rests on the fact that in times of conflict between a Basseri and a sedentary individual, the mere fact of the Basseri's nomadism puts him at a disadvantage. He must move on, or his herds cannot graze; he must move on, or will be effectively cut off from his entire community, who will move on without him. A farmer can ask neighbors to watch over property, or leave fields unattended; a nomad cannot. A farmer may go to court, and wait for his case to be heard; a nomad cannot.

The fact that the chief does not maintain a nomadic lifestyle becomes of paramount importance. He is not a stranger passing through. He is not a man of lowly means. As the powerful representative of any individual in the tribe, he is invaluable to each and every member. It is he who mediates the nomads' congress with the sedentary society which surrounds them, and can develop the friendly relations and alliances that the mobile tribe cannot

Relationships with outsiders

The individual Basseri rarely comes in contact with outsiders. Congress is most likely to occur when an animal has strayed and must be sought out in areas occupied by others. However, chiefs <u>do</u> have occasion to come together with chiefs of hostile tribes, and it is of some political importance that they do so. Such visits function to negotiate access to pastures in advance, so as to forestall any fighting of camp members along the migratory route.

Large decorative tents are erected for these occasions, and large communal hunts are arranged to procure game meat. Lavish meals and entertainment are provided, and such occasions are regarded as the most eagerly anticipated events of the year.

Other events which are particularly entertaining are trips to bazaars and markets. The purpose of these forays is to sell livestock and purchase clothes and luxury items. Most of the supplies that Basseri must purchase are not obtained at market, however. Each individual has trading relationships with a number of sedentary people living along the annual route

ECONOMIC ORGANIZATION

The complete attention of the Basseri people is focused on the most important feature of their economy: the herds. Their daily concerns are to foster the health and well-being of the animals, to ensure that they grow and reproduce, to avoid the risks (predominantly environmental) that place them in jeopardy. Drought, frosts, insects, and veterinary illness all threaten to decimate the herds, and by extension the herders, whose economic survival is invested in the animals.

This constant ongoing focus leaves them little time (nor, perhaps, inclination) to attempt to manipulate other features of their environment. For example, in the southern part of there territory are several areas of pasture which, although they hold great potential, are never used. The Basseri admit that this land would be superlative for pasturing were there only a water source for the animals close by. This could be accomplished with relative

ease: all these pasture lands could be made usable by the digging of a well. But this is not a project for small, autonomous households to undertake. It requires an organized communal effort. In contemplating this, Barth (1964:102) asks: "who would tend their flocks while they were engaged in the work, and why should one particular camp do it, when the fruits of the labour would be reaped by dozens of other camps as well?"

Thus, it is the animals on which they concentrate. As an individual herd grows, and the wealth of the owner increases, there comes a point at which, ironically, his capital is less secure. This is owing to the inability of an owner, whose herd has grown so large that it is impossible for him to oversee his shepherds effectively, to prevent theft and carelessness. Basseri say they are aware that s shepherd will not watch a flock under contract with the same vigilance he gives to his own; with a large herd, he can appropriate several animals and say they were lost; he can keep or sell dairy products without the owner knowing that he is diminishing the yield. Therefore, it is to the wealthy herd owners advantage to convert his wealth in livestock to other, less risky forms of wealth. He may purchase jewelry or carpets, or in the best of circumstances, land.

Along their migratory route, nomads can purchase plots which they then lease to sedentary villagers living in the area. The advantages of this are two-fold: not only does it allow the Basseri herder a more secure form of wealth, it also affords him great social status in the sedentary society outside the tribe. Basseri purchase land without any intent of settling on it; they are more interested in being able to obtain a portion of the agricultural yield, which they would otherwise have to purchase. Inevitably, however, there are always some landowners whose wealth becomes more and more invested in land, and who grows less interested in his herd and his traditional lifestyle. These individuals compromise by settling on their land for half the year, and spend the other half camping in tents near their former il-rah.

Sedentarization

It has been suggested that sedentarization of populations like the Basseri is often in response to the growth experienced by many tribes. (Barth 1964) Certainly accumulation of wealth, in the form of land, contributes to this process. Tremendous accumulation is forestalled when men have sons: much of this capital will be drained off via the custom of anticipated inheritance when sons marry. Therefore, such cumulative growth over a lifespan can really only accrue to fathers of daughters or men with no children at all. It is in this way that lack of male heirs can lead to wealth-induced sedentarization for some households.

On the other end of the scale is sedentarization by impoverishment, which is more often the case. Loss of ones herd may result in the inability to continue the pursuit of a nomadic lifestyle. Thus, too few animals may also result in a family being left behind, their only recourse being to adopt a sedentary lifestyle.

RELIGION AND EXPRESSIVE CULTURE

The Basseri are Shiah Moslems, and practice Islam in a less formal manner than some. They are, according to Barth (1964:135) "indifferent" to what he terms "metaphysical problems," and for the most part uninterested in religion.

There are no ritual specialists among the tribe, and upon the occasion of an uninvited visit by people with sacred status, the nomads are as likely to offer ridicule as gifts.

A village mullah (holy man) is likely to be asked to perform marriage ceremonies. Otherwise, Basseri ceremonials are tied to the cycle of seasons, life cycle events, and a few special ritual situations.

Knowledge of the events of the Moslem year are hazy at best, despite the reminders they encounter as they travel through observant villages. Customs are embraced haphazardly, prayer is infrequent and always a solitary act. While Islamic

feast days are taken into consideration when migration is being planned, they are not observed by the Basseri. The single deference to the Moslem calendar is in its influence on good luck or misfortune: no sheep shearing is practiced on Moslem holidays, and certain tasks of flock will not be undertaken on Friday, the Moslem sabbath.

By far it is the solar year which is of greater import to the Basseri, because it is on this division of time that the chief plans migration. Celebrations that mark the beginning of a new season or a new year are noted, although there are no elaborate observances that would interfere with packing up the camp and moving on as usual.

Since the migrations are of an annual nature, it is around the yearly cycle that Basseri organize their life and their conceptualization of time. There are shrines set up along the route which mark the graves of important or holy men. They are shown respect when passed by, but have no ceremony, myth, or ritual attached to their acknowledgment. The single exception to this is a shrine which nearly all the camps' migratory routes take them past, and where a stopover is often planned. Animals may be sacrificed and eaten at the site, but the ambiance is one of festivity rather than reverence or solemnity (Barth 1964).

More elaborated are those rituals performed on the occasions of marriages, births and deaths.

The birth of a child (especially a first born) is an occasion for great celebration, with sweets given and the noise of rifles fired in the air. For the first three days of life, and weekly for more than a month, an infant is cut with razor blades on the nose, neck and chest. (Later in childhood, children are cut on the ears to prevent earache.) This is a measure to prevent a child's blood from becoming polluted later on--a circumstance disclosed by an adolescent's pimples.

Boys are circumcised in infancy by village physicians (or barbers) if travel allows. If not, this is put off until the boy is six or seven, since it is believed that before this age the procedure would be frightening to him. No analagous ritual is performed for girls.

Sexual activity is strictly forbidden before marriage, and when adolescents are found meeting in secret to kiss, girls will generally be beaten. These early romances, which almost never progress past these innocent stages even without discovery, have no bearing on betrothal or marriage, which is arranged without regard for the inclinations of the future bride and groom.

Marriage is perhaps the most elaborate of all ceremonials, with ritual feasting, bathing of the bride and groom, and participation of neighboring camps. The bride and groom are each prepared inn separate ritual tents, where they are shaved, bathed and oiled. After the ceremony they retire to the bridal tent, where a guard stands by, rifle in hand, which he will shoot off to alert the community that the marriage has been consummated. The bridal sheets are inspected for the blood believed to signal that the bride was a virgin. If it is not in evidence, the marriage may be immediately dissolved, with the groom under no obligation to give back the dowry (and, often, with the bride price returned to his family).

Death and burial are attended by minimal ceremony. Household members will spend several hours in their tent, grieving, and the body will be immediately buried in a village cemetery. Before burial, the body is washed and if there is a relative of the deceased who knows the appropriate section of the Koran to chant, this will be done. The atmosphere is not one of expressive mourning, but rather of silence and solemnity. Sorrow and love for the deceased is expressed by gifts of sweets every Friday for what may be an extended period of time. Relatives may become quite emotional on subsequent treks which allow them to visit the gravesite of the deceased, and it is not uncommon for family members to approach the cemetery with weeping and chanting.

Apart from seasonal and life cycle observances are actions and avoidances which are designed to promote good luck and avoid misfortune and the evil eye.

Most of the beliefs surrounding good and bad luck pertain to actions with their animals: which ones should not be together during shearing, what practices should be avoided during milking. Beliefs about the evil eye, which derives from envy, are more pervasive but less specific in their proscriptions. This may be because its consequences are thought to be less avoidable. There is no cure for the ills it brings, and it acts out of the awareness of the person in whom it resides.

Envious thoughts on the part of any individual may result in the illness or death of the individual envied. All people have the potential to harbor this power, although those with blue eyes are particularly suspect.

Since spontaneous thoughts of envy may come unbidden into anyone's mind, precautions are taken to distract the onlooker from the potential object of envy, usually a child or animal. This may be accomplished by decorations tied around the animal's leg, or baby's neck, in the hopes that they will signal caution to the person who may unintentionally think covetous thoughts.

Barth (1964) remarks on what seems to be a striking dearth of ritual and expressive culture among the Basseri, but concludes that this assessment may be in error. While there is surely less ceremonial practice and elaborate display than is found among many other peoples, for the Basseri their movement is their ceremony. That the activities of their days are practical should not eliminate them out of hand for consideration as deeply meaningful. As their il-rah unfolds before them and they journey through the seasons and through their year, they are, in effect, celebrating their very existence.

BASSERI

REFERENCES

BARTH, F.
    1964   *Nomads of South
              Persia*.Oslo:
              Universitetsforlaget.

SALZMAN, P.C.
    1974   Political Organization
              among Nomadic People.
              in *Man in Adaptation*.
              Y.A. Cohen, ed.
              Chicago:Aldine.

§ THE BEGINNING

"When the land came into form" there were no trees, there were no animals, there were no streams, there was no food. But there were people. People covered the earth. The people had no food, and so they were hungry. They had no homes, so they were cold. One stood up and gathered all the people together. He told one group to be trees, and they became trees. He told one group to be fish, and they became fish. He told one group to be banana, and sago, and finally all the plants and animals, rivers and hills, were there. The few who were left became the human beings. (Schieffelin 1976)

INTRODUCTION AND HISTORY

The Kaluli live in the tropical rainforest in the Southern Highlands Province of Papua New Guinea on the Great Papuan Plateau. They are the most numerous of four related horticultural groups who collectively call themselves Bosavi kalu, "people of Bosavi." The addition of the suffix -li (real) makes the meaning of Kaluli "real people."

The Bosavi people, whose number has been approximated from 1200 to 2000, live in about 20 longhouse communities built on ridges throughout the dense forest. Each community is about an hours walk from the next, and the vegetation is nearly unbroken between them.

Although there are signs suggesting that the Kaluli are perhaps more closely related to lowland groups than to their closer neighbors in the New Guinea highlands, Bosavi tell no stories of their people coming to their present land from somewhere else. Their mythology tells that they have always lived on the plateau. Over the past several generations they have been slowly moving eastward into unsettled, more heavily forested terrain. This movement may be a search for better gardening lands, an attempt to escape enemies, or to flee epidemics with which they have had to contend.

Kaluli traded extensively with friendly neighbors, but it was in the middle 1930s that the first Europeans visited the Great Papuan Plateau, bringing trade goods that had never been encountered. Chief among these were steel axes and knives, mirrors, beads, and pearl shells. World War II intervened, and European contact was broken until the 1950s. Between these two times, however, disaster struck the plateau in the form of measles and influenza epidemics. The populations of several groups were decimated, with the loss of lives ranging from thirty percent to, in some places, seventy percent of the population. The Kaluli lost fully one quarter of their population. This threat is ongoing: despite public health programs, infant mortality is high and influenza epidemics still sweep the lowlands annually, resulting in a slowly declining population rate.

In the 1960s and 1970s the impact of evangelical Christianity could be seen in Kaluli communities. Schieffelin (1976) reports that earlier attempts by Seventh Day Adventist missionaries were unsuccessful. When it was learned that this religion forbade eating pork, it was concluded that the minister was crazy and he was forced to abandon his mission.

The life of the land

It is significant that longhouse identity is associated more with the land on which it sits than the clan affiliation of the people within. The name of a community's land becomes an integral part of their identity, and it is invoked in both friendly and hostile interactions. It is used much like a name in friendly socializing; in war these place names served other purposes. Enemies on the attack were on unfamiliar turf, with no knowledge of which ridges and trails might be well suited for defenders to hide behind in ambush. As they raced into battle, those defending their home territory hurled names of landmarks like weapons; these were met with the frantic cries of the enemies' own territorial names. Those that identified places of past victories were particularly powerful. Such a display was effective because it took advantage of the fright assumed to be felt by parties who were on strange land, who were someplace they didn't belong.

In both these uses of place names--to identify themselves in friendly conversation and to verbally attack their enemies in battle--Kaluli are demonstrating how much their land is part of themselves. Edward Schieffelin, an anthropologist who has spent much time with the Kaluli, says it was explained to him this way: "When a man lives somewhere for a long time...his name is in the ground just like you put your name in that book." (1976:44) Often as he walked through the forest with informants, one would point to a faintly discernible spot where the trees were thinner and remark that he had lived there as a small boy. A patch of weeds or remnant of a wooden post would be identified, the individual remarking casually on whose garden or house it had been. Schieffelin came to understand that these places held for the Kaluli the content of their past; they call themselves by their place because they see themselves in their land.

The Kaluli mark time in a predominantly seasonal way. Their terms for seasonal change and the progression of time are not based on changes in weather, however, or phases of the moon, but rather are based on changes in forest vegetation. These changes are further demarcated by changes in the bird population. The appearance of a particular bird during the month of April hearkens the onset of a time which lasts through September, and is often heralded by enthusiastic cries that the season is "really here: we heard 'bili'", the bird which appears at this time, a comment sounding much like our "first robin of Spring." Days, too, are apportioned by the birds--

the morning calls of one wake the children; the late-afternoon sounds of another alert people to come sit together for their meal. Not only time, but also space may be demarcated by birds. Their eating or nesting places may be used to describe portions of villages or trails, or to indicate direction.

SETTLEMENTS

The patrilocal village is made up of men belonging to the lineages of several patrilineal clans, along with their wives, children, and other female relatives. Relationships between villages are maintained by ties of marriage and matrilineal affiliation.

Each Kaluli community is structured with one longhouse and several smaller houses centered around a clearing. The longhouse is the main residence; smaller houses function more as temporary shelters for families from the longhouse who live nearer the gardens when it is time to harvest. A large longhouse may be sixty by thirty feet, with porches built onto either end. The entire structure is built up off the ground from five to twelve feet, and supported by poles. This elevation provides the best vantage point from which to see enemy raiders. Surrounding forests are cut down to enhance visibility, and the cavernous space left beneath the longhouse is inhabited by domesticated pigs, whose noise at the approach of strangers makes them effective "watchdogs."

The interior of the longhouse is divided in half by a hall running down its length. On either side are the men's sleeping platforms, made of bark and raised a foot or so off the ground. Near each is a firebox used for curing meat, and piles of firewood and smoked game are heaped near them. Other foods and possessions are hung by strings from the rafters, to keep them out of the reach of rats. Women, children, and piglets not yet consigned to the space beneath the longhouse sleep in closer quarters in passageways running down the sides of the house. Elderly men and unmarried youths occupy one corner of these, and older women of prestige along with unmarried girls share a section of the women's area.

Individual fireboxes are used for smaller, solitary meals or "snacks"; but the longhouse functions as much as a town hall as it does a residence. When there are important matters to discuss, visitors to entertain, or important ceremonial occasions, the community fireboxes in the central hallway are the focal point. In all, about fifteen families, usually totaling about sixty people, reside in each longhouse. It is the longhouse community, more so than any other tie that engenders feelings of loyalty in the Kaluli. People usually refer to themselves by the location of their longhouse rather than that of their clan. The residents build their house and plant their gardens together. They hunt and fish, sing and cook, in unison. When a youth is to be married, most longhouse residents contribute to the brideprice; when a gift of meat is received, it is shared with co-residents.

While it may seem as if living in the longhouse would be cramped and engender squabbling, this is usually not the case because families are often absent from the longhouse for weeks at a time. Small houses near garden sites, while certainly temporary shelters, are used often in two and three week blocks. At times when their own gardens are less demanding, families may travel to other longhouse communities to assist clan members with their own planting and gardening. In addition to local travel and gardening chores, hunting and trading expeditions take Kaluli away from the longhouses for extended periods of time. Old longhouses give way to new ones when gardens become exhausted. After two or three years longhouses fall into disrepair, and the residents plant new gardens and construct a new longhouse. Often the old structure is used less and less, as the garden fails, until finally it is abandoned and the new structure becomes permanent.

KALULI

ECONOMIC AND POLITICAL ORGANIZATION

In several ways, Kaluli society stands in great contrast to other groups in the New Guinea Highlands.

Both politically and economically, Kaluli society is highly egalitarian. Not only are there no formal positions of leadership, there is also no role of Big Man, the wealthy individual who rises to an informal position of great influence found so widely among other highland groups.

Absent too the highland pattern of elaborate exchange for personal wealth. Whether exchange be formal and ceremonial or in the context of everyday activity, Kaluli do not use it as an occasion for enhancing status. Exchanges generally engaged in elsewhere in the region revolve primarily around life-cycle events and political activity. The most significant occasion of formal exchange in Kaluli society is marriage.

Subsistence activities

The Kaluli are intimately familiar with the land they garden. Individual trees, hills and streams are all referred to by their own names. Not only forest growth, but also inhabitants and travelers are recognizable: Kaluli can identify the footprints not only of one another, but of individual pigs.

Kaluli practice swidden horticulture in extensive gardens, and have a rich and varied diet. Their daily staple food is sago, a starch which they extract from wild sago palms that grow along streams a short walk from each village. Bananas, pandanus, breadfruit, sugarcane, sweet potatoes and green vegetables from their gardens supplement the sago eaten at every meal. Most of the daily protein is gathered casually, by scooping up a small crayfish from underneath a rock, or dipping a hand into a brook for a small fish. Small rodents or lizards darting across a Kaluli's path will be stabbed with a stick or summarily stamped underfoot.

There are fish in abundance in numerous rivers and streams throughout the area, and small game is easily come by in surrounding forests. The Kaluli may venture on a several day trip to unsettled forests where game is more abundant, but usually these treks are reserved for times when larger amounts of game are needed for an exchange. A small number of domestic pigs are kept. Forest foods are in dependable supply, particularly owing to the low population density.

Trade and Manufacture

Kaluli trade both with other groups and within their own community of Kaluli. While they have the most long-standing trade relationships with people to the north, trade has been more recently established with those living in the east. Each of several important trade routes was characterized by its own specific items. From the people in the west they secured hornbill beaks and strings of dogs teeth; from the south came tree oil. To these items they added their own net bags, and traded all of these to the highland Huli. In return the Huli provided salt, tobacco, and aprons woven from net.

Trade between longhouse groups was active, and relationships between the longhouses were forged by chains of marital alliances. These marriage ties and trading relations afforded the opportunity to travel between communities with hospitality assured, as well as provide allies when needed for conflict resolution.

Kaluli manufacture tools for gardening, stone adzes, bows from palm trees, and net bags. The forest provides materials for constructing longhouses and fences. The most elaborate items of manufacture are the extravagant costumes created for important ceremonial occasions.

Division of labor

While the everyday activities of men and women are separate, and male and female gender roles are clearly differentiated, there is among the Kaluli none of hostility between men and women often reported in the New Guinea highlands. Daily activities of labor and socialization are cooperative, and men and women are more complementary than competitive.

Women tend the gardens, look after the pigs, "hunt" small forest game and gather other small protein sources. They are responsible for processing the staple starch, sago. It is to woman that the important task of socializing the children is primarily entrusted.

Men often organize their labor as group activity, drawing on their networks of reciprocity and obligation to accomplish the strenuous tasks of cutting down and dividing trees, clearing large garden plots, building dams and fences, and planting.

Conflict and control

Given that there is no formal system of control in the absence of a leader with the authority to enforce rules and exact punishment, it is left to methods of informal sanction. Usually this is accomplished through gossip or ostracism. A person who has strayed outside the boundaries of personal or social parameters may be confronted by the injured parties and asked for compensation. Strong beliefs in the power of the supernatural to redress violations of taboos function as an effective deterrent to misbehavior. In the past, the anticipation of enemy raids as retaliation was quite effective too, but in recent years this activity has been disallowed by the government. Schieffelin (1976) reports that rather than feeling resentment towards this official outside interference, most Kaluli are instead relieved that the danger inherent in the old days of retaliatory murder was gone.

The usual causes of conflict among the Kaluli are theft and death. It is the latter that, before government sanction, gave rise to intense violence. Deaths are believed to result from witchcraft; it was the offending witch who was the object of the counterattack. Witches are still held accountable for their actions, but are not routed out of their longhouses and clubbed to death. Compensation of another sort is requested, although without formal sanctions in place such payment cannot be assured.

SOCIAL ORGANIZATION

Kinship and descent

Kaluli are organized into exogamous, patrilineal clans that are scattered throughout all the longhouse communities. In any single longhouse there resides the localized lineages of two or more clans. Even though clan membership is conferred through the male line, each Kaluli individual claims kinship to both mother's and father's groups. Paternal kin provides those ties within the residential longhouse; maternal ties connect an individual to relatives living in other longhouses. The group of individuals to whom one feels closest--those with whom one has grown up, or sees most often--take food from each others gardens, and share food in return. More distant kin (with distance in this case being two or more generations away) are lumped together with the same term ("grandparent" or "grandchild") used to refer to people who are no relation at all.

The most important tie in establishing relationships, however, is that of sibship. Siblings, among the Kaluli, are those who are ones actual siblings as well as parallel cousins (mother's sister's children and father's brother's children).

Marriage

The preferred Kaluli marriage is one in which the man and woman belong to different clans, and refer to one another with the term reserved for distant kin and unrelated individuals.

Arrangements for marriage are instigated by the elders in the groom's longhouse, often quite without his knowledge. A woman is selected and the bridewealth collected, all unbeknownst to the couple. Schieffelin (1976) remarks that by the time arrangements are nearing completion, the groom is often the last to know, and his closest friends delight in being the ones to shock him with the news.

Marriage sets in motion a life-long relationship of exchange. A formal relationship is begun with the collection and bestowal of bridewealth. Friends and relatives of the groom contribute goods, thereby solidifying their previous relationship with the groom, and establishing a new one with the bride. This relationship involves the usual extension of food and hospitality that one might ordinarily expect from kin; but it further binds the contributors to the ongoing state of the couple's marriage. If the wife should die as a result of witchcraft, a bridewealth contributor seeks revenge. Should a woman commit adultery, he supports the husband in his dispute. In the event of the husband's death, contributors "officially" have the right to give their opinion on the fate of the children, but this option is rarely exercised. The relationship comes full circle when the friends and kin who contributed to the original bridewealth receive part of the bridewealth of the couples' daughters, commensurate to that which they contributed long ago.

The compensation inherent in bridewealth is both in recognition of the nurturance provided by her family as she grew, but also for loss: loss of the daughter they love, who will go away with her husband, and loss of her important contributions to the economy of their own longhouse. Especially affected are the girl's unmarried brothers, for whom she has labored domestically much in the way a wife would. While the ideal compensation is the groom's donation of a sister to the bride's family, such so-called "sister exchange" doesn't occur with great

frequency. Another function of bridewealth payment is to describe the universe of in-laws as those who have received part of the payment.

SOCIALIZATION

The socialization of children in Kaluli society has been elegantly described by Bambi Schieffelin (1990), a linguistic anthropologist who weaves the general socialization of children together with the teaching of language.

Girls and boys

One of the first social lessons children learn is the appropriate content of their sex roles. Since it is the mother who interacts most intensively with her children, the task of emphasizing the child's sex, taken up in the first days of life, falls to her. Whether she and the child are alone or surrounded by others, she calls attention to the child's sex by the way she structures the content of her conversation and interaction.

Sons are told how strong they will one day be. Mothers structure games and other activities that employ aggression and assertive behavior. Boys are expressly taught that they will get what they want if they are endlessly demanding, and never give up their pursuit. They are taught to beg, to wheedle, and even to have vigorous tantrums until their needs are finally met. They are expected to perfect the talents that will ensure that it is both their behavior and their wishes that will be attended to.

Daughters are taught something very different. While all young children are recognized to be naturally "helpless," girls are not permitted to maintain this pose for very long. Unlike boys, who are endlessly needy and always on the receiving end, girls are assigned chores to do as soon as they are physically coordinated enough to begin to manage them. Their activities are those that are designed to serve others; daily they fetch firewood, carry water, weed gardens. In addition to this sort of labor, their nurturing skills are an important focus of girls' socialization. As soon as a new baby is born, a little girl becomes an older sister, which is a role of extreme importance in Kaluli life. She already knows that her own wants are secondary to those of others; when her mother presents her with a new sibling, this lesson is intensified.

(In fact, so special is the relationship of an older sister to her younger brother, that in order to facilitate his integration into the community, Steven Feld, an anthropologist studying Bosavi music, was introduced to the community by Schieffelin as her younger brother. The Kaluli welcomed him warmly as her sibling.)

As will be elaborated later, sharing plays a critical role in Bosavi social life. For any Kaluli to say , "I have none" is such a basic strategy that it is a named kind of talk (gesema, 'make one feel sorrow or pity') and usually results in the receipt of whatever goods were lacking. Saying this conveys to the potential donor, "You have something I don't; I want it, and have rightful claim to it; you must give me some, while feeling sorry I have none." This basic mode of expression is elaborated in a boy's relationship with his older sister, as he is taught explicitly the proper whining and begging appeal with which to approach her.

"Hardening" language and behavior

It is recognized that all children--not just boys--are naturally dependent when they are small. Children, it seems, are always hungry; they beg and whine for food endlessly. Adults feel pity at such plaintive appeals and children are never denied.

But children cannot continue indefinitely in this vein. They are thought to beg and whine "naturally;" they must learn other important forms of communication socially. And this they learn through lessons in language.

Reciprocity and sharing are the anchors of Kaluli life, and it is important that children learn to participate in a variety of important social exchanges. It is through learning appropriate language that children become participants in all varieties of social exchange. Although they may start out as helpless, by they time they are three years old, children are expected to be able to be join in reciprocity--to be able to give as well as receive, and to ask and offer with the proper words.

Babies are thought of as "soft." They are unable to understand what is said around them, they have no control over their bodies' movement or function; they are loose and "floppy." Children's early physical and mental development parallel one another: both are conceptualized as "firming up." Not only must they become more physically sturdy and socially assertive; they must also "firm up" their language, and be taught to be articulate members of their speech community. The process of a child's mind and body maturing together is called "hardening." When Schieffelin, raising her own small child among the Kaluli, asked for some indicators that such a process was in fact taking place, she was told that sometimes one can count a child's teeth as a marker of developmental stage; teeth allow for more exact speech.

"Hardening" of children puts them in control of themselves and others. Mothers actively guide their children in language use that will "harden" them. They tell their toddlers what to say and how to say it in "hard" language. Asking for something in the child's "natural" language of whining and cajoling must be supplanted by the hard way of asking for what one needs. This is important preparation for a life based on sharing and exchange. Once a child can use hard language to ask, then others may do the same and ask the child to share with them. Thus, a child can be drawn into the important activity of sharing with others in the household. The aim of socialization, therefore, is not only to "harden" them physically and mentally; once they have been hardened linguistically, they can be responsible members of the community.

The qualities of "hard" and "soft" are ones that go beyond the realm of childhood development. The world was once a soft place, until the mud was stamped on and made hard. A "hard" man is one who is strong and outspoken--who possesses the skill of using hard language.

In song and ceremony, key elements of Kaluli culture, a successful performance is one which brings the audience to tears. To have this facility in singing and composition is to "harden" the song, and only a "hardened" performance is a skillful one.

"Soft" things are likened to weakness and decay. Things that are "soft" can in fact be dangerous, in that they can impede the process of hardening. Children (thought to be themselves "soft") must never eat eggs, which are mushy, or any foods which are yellow, a color which symbolizes frailty and spoilage. They must also avoid the meat of birds whose high-pitched calls are "soft."

THE GIVING AND SHARING OF FOOD

The muni bird

A girl and her younger brother set off to a stream together to catch crayfish; while the girl soon was successful, her brother had made no catch. He whined to his sister, "I have no crayfish," but her reply was that he could not have hers, as it was for their mother. Soon she caught a second but her brother still had none, and again whined for hers and was again refused: it is for father. Upon her third catch her younger brother begged for the crayfish, only to be told it was for their older brother. Shortly after, the young boy caught a tiny shrimp, whose shell he placed on his nose, turning it bright red. As he looked at his hands, which held the meat of the shrimp, they became red wings. His older sister, frightened at her brother's transformation into a bird, begged him not to fly away. His reply was only the high, mournful cry of the muni bird he had become, as he flew off. Weeping, his sister called to him to take the crayfish she had caught, take them all, eat them all, but his song only continued; crying, he sang that he had no sister and he was hungry. (Feld 1990)

The giving and sharing of food is perhaps the most fundamental theme in Kaluli interpersonal relations. It promotes friendship and familiarity; it is a vehicle for showing fondness.

Food is an avocation, an interest beyond mere survival. At times when he has no chores which need accomplishing, a man will stroll to his gardens to check the growth of his fruits, or make some other observation about the gathering of grubs or other food preparation.

Food is one of the primary ways of relating to children. They can be calmed, made unafraid of new faces, and shown affection all by the offer of food. Even as little as a day after their birth, Kaluli babies will be taken to the forest for several days' fishing and grub gathering. Newborns will be fed these gathered treats both to make them strong as well as to welcome them into this world and urge them not to return to the place from which they came. Such sharing of food with a baby allows a child's father and other family members to forge the crucial bond made by feeding which would otherwise be exclusive to the baby and breast-feeding mother.

This sets in motion the lifelong Kaluli pattern of sharing food as a form of sharing affection. A small piece of meat or portion of salt is an unequivocal declaration of feeling from one unmarried adolescent to another, and the exclamation, "He gave me pork!" is a heartfelt expression of the depth of loss felt after the death of a friend. (Schieffelin 1976:48)

Sharing of food is the expected norm. When one family within the longhouse cooks, it is understood that all who are hungry will have some. Likewise, when one is in need of extra shoots to plant in a garden, or food at mealtime, it is expected that one will be provided for. This is especially true when the food in question is a delicacy, such as game meat.

At times when food is not, or cannot be, shared, Kaluli manners dictate that it should be consumed discretely. Even if there is no greedy intent, excluded individuals are to be sheltered from any offense this might engender. For example, men eating fish of a kind taboo to their wives and children will be considerate enough to do so out of the sight of their families.

Anthropologist Edward Schieffelin, at the beginning of his years among the Kaluli, found that when he could enlist no aid from individuals for even double the expected wages, he could entice them to help for a cup of rice or a tin of meat. He reminds us that this interest in food does not derive from the lack of it. The importance of food is found in its use as a focus of social relations. Schieffelin (1976) explains: "I became aware of this as soon as I entered a longhouse on the plateau for the first time. I sat down wearily on the edge of the men's sleeping platform and was pulling leeches out of my socks when a man approached with a blackened, loaf-shaped packet in his hand. He broke off a piece and handed me a chalky-looking substance covered with grayish, rubbery skin. There was a pause while the people of the longhouse watched to see what I would do. Reluctantly, I took a bite. The flavor was strongly reminiscent of plaster of paris. 'Nafa?' ('Good?') asked one of my hosts hopefully, using one of the few Kaluli words I knew at the time. 'Nafa,' I answered when I could get some saliva back in my mouth. 'Ah,' said my host, looking around to the others. They relaxed. Having eaten sago, I was established as a fellow creature." (p. 47)

Kaluli do not share food because of the obligations of a relationship as much as to solidify and actualize the relationship through the giving of food. As Schieffelin (1976:63) explains, "it is through giving and sharing food that the relationship becomes socially real." In fact, the true definition of a mother, for the Kaluli, is less the woman who gives birth to a child as the one who feeds a child. By extension, if a woman feeds a child over some period of time her children "become" that child's siblings.

In the myth of the boy who became a muni bird, told above, we can identify several of what have now become familiar Kaluli themes--the sharing of food, the responsibility of a sister to her brother, the opposing postures of pleading boys and nurturing girls, and birds and their sad sounds.

A young boy, plaintiff and whining in an appropriate manner, asks his older sister for what among the Kaluli should be his due: denying a child food is unthinkable. For an older sister to deny food, three times, to her younger brother runs counter to the most basic Kaluli social norms. As the younger brother is denied food by his older sister, he ceases to be her brother; even more--he is, in fact, no longer a person at all.

Birth and death, illness and health, mourning and joy all have mandates and taboos revolving around foodstuffs. The reason given for the Kaluli's appropriation of food as the ultimate vehicle for constructing social relationships and expressing affection is that food is cornerstone of life. If food shows affection, then what does it mean to go hungry? It means more than an empty belly: it means loneliness.

RELIGION AND EXPRESSIVE CULTURE

The unseen world

All that cannot be seen is a very real part of Kaluli life. The forest is thick and hides many things from the eyes, but is full of sound. The skittering flight and screech of a bird tells you of someone approaching as precisely as catching sight of the visitor does. Morning is not sunrise, but birdsong. Evening is not dusk, but cicadas. Schieffelin (1976) was unable to convey to a Kaluli friend the kind of bird whose name he wanted to know, however detailed his report. But when he remembered the rattle of its wings and crumpled a piece of paper in description, the bird was immediately recognized.

These sounds are not merely sounds. When a Kaluli draws attention to the mournful call of a pigeon, saying that it is a little child calling for its mother, it may in fact be just that. It is not only that the bird's call sounds that way; there are spirits that live unseen, and indeed the soul of a child may call for its mother. (It is not unusual that birds and their sounds are prime examples of the importance to the Kaluli of what is heard. They hold a prominent place in Kaluli life, as we will see.)

There are people in the unseen world who are called with a term meaning "shadow" or "reflection." In this unseen world every person has a shadow. Shadows of men are wild pigs; shadows of women are cassowaries. These shadows lead their own lives in the unseen world, roaming the forests. Should the shadow be hurt, the person would suffer too. If the shadow is killed, it means death for its Kaluli counterpart.

Spirits of the dead also live in this unseen world, along with spirits who have never had a human life. These are not fearful sorts of spirits; on the contrary, they might once have been friends or relatives. Unlike other New Guinea peoples, the Kaluli think it impossible that the dead would bear the living any ill will.

There are large invisible longhouses on Mt. Bosavi which are home to another sort of spirit, quite different from the spirits of the dead. As humans have spirit reflections that are wild pigs and cassowaries, so these "people" have the reciprocal spirit: their shadows are the wild pigs and cassowaries that live in Bosavi. These shadows are not evil, but they are responsible for dangerous thunderstorms.

There is, however, a third kind of spirit, which lives in certain well-known areas of the land and whose anger can only be prevented by taking certain precautions. These shadows are dangerous, and may send foul weather, sickness and even death.

Mediums and witches

It is through mediums that Kaluli have knowledge of the unseen world. Men who have married spirit women in a dream gain access to this world when they have a child with their spirit wife. As the medium sleeps he leaves his body behind and wanders the unseen world. Once he has gone, spirits can enter his body and use his mouth to speak to the living.

Such seances are exciting occasions for Kaluli who wish to speak to departed loved ones. They are eager to learn what animal form friends and relatives have taken in the unseen world, inquire if they have enough to eat, and ask advice about curing the sick and locating lost property. They also petition their help to identify the seis, witches who live among them in the community.

Every Kaluli death, whatever the outward cause may appear to be (old age, illness, an accident), is caused by a sei, a term used to describe both an evil spirit and the person whom the spirit inhabits. Seis are usually men, but sometimes women, who have an evil spirit lodged in their heart about which they themselves may be unaware. While they sleep, the shadow creature that dwells within them stalks the night for prey. A sei typically attacks only strangers, but hunger or anger can cause him to turn on his own kin.

Although the seis are generally unseen, some on their deathbed or with particular abilities have in fact seen them, and describe them as hideous. Their attacks leave sickness and disability which is often as invisible as they are: a painful, distended belly contains unseen stones; legs that cannot move have been amputated by the sei, but can still be seen. When the victim is fully compromised, the sei will pull out his victim's heart, killing him. Once the prey is dead, the sei will finish eating the rest of his body. This is evidenced by a corpse's ongoing decomposition and eventual disappearance.

Death and Afterlife

At death, a person's spirit is freed from the still body and retreats to the forest . There it begins a journey along a river, which to the spirit is a wide westward path, only to arrive at an enormous bonfire where it burns until finding deliverance in another spirit. This rescuer carries the burnt soul back to its own spirit longhouse, attending healing ceremonies along the way until the restoration is complete. Finally, the two are married. After this union the newly departed will assume a new form, and will resemble any other wild creature in the forest. Loved ones will not see it again, but may look forward to conversation and advice through a medium.

Traditional mortuary practices have been outlawed by the government, which now requires that Kaluli bury bodies in a cemetery. Prior to this edict, issued in 1968, the body would be placed in a hammock outside the long house, with fires lit around it. Mourners would come for several days; afterwards the body was removed to a small structure built near the longhouse, where it would decompose. Small possessions treasured by the deceased would be placed there with him, as sentimental reminders. These were not meant to travel to the afterlife with their former owner: what use would a wild pig in the forest, or a bird soon to live in a treetop have for a necklace or bow and arrow?

Once only bones remained, they would be gathered into a net bag and placed under the eaves of the longhouse front porch.

The children and spouse of the deceased were required to follow several taboos established for mourners; often others did so too, simply out of affection. If a woman has gathered food to eat with another before her own death, her intended companion might refuse to eat it, sad that they could not share it together as they had planned. One man gave up breadfruit upon his brother's death, because it had been his brother's favorite food. (Schieffelin 1976).

STORY, SONG, AND CEREMONY

Songs of birds, sounds of tears

Steven Feld was an anthropology student making a living as a jazz musician while he pondered the question of returning to school to complete his degree. At the home of his friends, anthropologists Edward and Bambi Schieffelin, he heard Kaluli music and was smitten. Deciding to merge his musical and anthropological interests, he went to Bosavi with the Schieffelins and studied sound--in the performance of poetry reading, song, and weeping--as a symbolic system.

Kaluli myth and music was the vehicle for his understanding of the way Kaluli relate to their world. Many Kaluli stories are about birds, and their connection with sadness, often due to the sorrowful nature of their calls. As Feld listened to such stories, he began to reflect upon similar associations in his own musical culture, especially American blues and jazz. He recalled "literary and musical imagery, such as the common use of the mournful sounds of the whippoorwill...in poetry and songs about sadness and love. ...By associating a bird of the night with minor or descending pitches, sad sounds, blacks, the South, and the beginning o f instrumental blues," (1990:23) Feld found a theme present in music and folklore in many diverse places He began then to regard the themes woven through Kaluli myth and the sounds repeated in Kaluli music as "expressive embodiments of basic Kaluli concepts of sentiment and appeal." (p.24)

Birds and their music are, for the Kaluli, who are avid bird-watchers, metaphors for their own society. It is most often birds that become the "spirit reflections" of the dead. Skillful at identifying birds by their sounds, Kaluli analogize the particular pitches and melodies of different birds with different

KALULI

segments of their population. (As when the whining and whimpering complaints of children are likened to that of the dove, whose call is said to be like that of "a hungry child calling for its mother.")

Once Feld discovered the centrality of birds and their songs to Kaluli culture, he proceeded to collect and organize all the information he could about the birds in the Bosavi environment, and the ways in which the Kaluli regarded them. This endeavor inadvertently taught him more than he anticipated: he expected to discover Kaluli notions of bird classification, perception, and symbolism. What he learned instead grew out of the sheer frustration of his Kaluli informant, who after hours of imitating bird calls and nesting behaviors blurted out, "Listen--to you they are birds, to me they are voices in the forest." Feld realized that he could not continue to impose his own system of classification on the Kaluli experience of these important "voices;" that the Kaluli understanding of birds and their songs is "based on certain fundamental premises about the world, such as the belief that things have a visible and invisible aspect; that sounds and behaviors have an outside, an inside, and an underneath; or that human relationships are reflected in the ecology and natural order of the forest." (p. 45)

Weeping conveys an emotional message from one person to another which is very much connected to singing. In response to sorrow or loss, Kaluli may begin to cry. But feelings of disappointment, frustration, or self-pity may also lead Kaluli to burst into song.

Weeping and singing are very much bound up together. There are many "wept songs," usually about a lost loved one. Men and women have different socially dictated modes of weeping. Men begin with a high pitched wail which turns into an imitation of the short-burst call of the muni bird. They cry for a short period of time, and stop abruptly. Weeping is a more common expressive form among women. While both men and women cry similarly in response to a moving song, it is women who are likely to blend weeping and singing into the sung text of a "wept song." As Feld (1990:33) explains, "while sadness moves both men and women to weeping, it is weeping that moves women to song."

Out of the attempt to preserve the musical heritage of the Kaluli, Feld has joined with other musicians to produce a recording of Bosavi music, *Voices of the Rainforest* . Profits from its sale benefit the Bosavi People's Fund, set up to provide financial aid in the struggle to maintain Kaluli cultural survival in the face of threats to their rainforest environment.

The gisaro

The usual occasions for Kaluli formal ceremonies are those they celebrate with neighboring longhouses: most often marriages or large gifts of meat. Pig feasts and similar large events take months to prepare.

Underlying these community events is the theme of reciprocity and exchange. After a particularly complex and moving ceremony, guests may be moved to host a return event in their own longhouse community in great haste. Schieffelin (1976) reports witnessing a dance performed to ward off sickness. Guest dancers from another village came to the host community, singing throughout the night, and performing so poignantly that it moved many to tears. As soon as the dancers departed, elders called in kin from other longhouses and within two days had staged a ceremony at the dancers' village that (they were proud to note) caused all assembled to weep.

Of all the ceremonies performed in Kaluli life, none is as important as the gisaro. It is presented as part of a larger ceremony (such as a wedding or pork prestation), and performed inside a host longhouse by guest dancers who begin at dusk and continue until dawn.

The cast is assembled by sending out requests to those who might like to participate, and it is rare that there are not enough men who respond to the call. For weeks before the event, gisaro dancers compose songs and prepare elaborate costumes. The intended effect of the gisaro performance is to overwhelm the listeners with powerful emotion. To this end, it is imperative to maintain the element of surprise, as to the identity of the dancers, pattern of makeup and costume, and content of the songs.

While the performers are rehearsing at least a dozen new songs and dances, the hosts are preparing food. On the day of the feast, dancers wait for dark and enter the longhouse which is lit with the torches soon to be a central part of the gisaro.

Gisaro dancers are painted and costumed alike, so as to be indistinguishable from one another. A rested dancer can thus replace an exhausted one, allowing the dancing and singing to continue unabated. The songs are heartbreaking, and purposely so. They tell of people and places loved and lost. The audience hangs on every word, their sorrow building until they can no longer contain themselves. Sobbing and wailing fills the longhouse, but the gisaro performers continue, seemingly oblivious to the anguish they are causing, never showing any trace of emotion on their faces.

Amid their wailing and stamping, hosts angered by the pain inflicted on them by the wrenching gisaro songs, jump up and grab the huge resin torches. These they jam into the back and neck of the dancer, searing his flesh. Still he continues, singing and dancing, as the enraged and grieving hosts continue to burn the dancers. The wailing and burning continues throughout the night.

Before the ceremony, dancers coat their bodies with sweet smelling vegetable resin whose scent mingles with the burning flesh. It is thought to afford the skin some protection from the burns and diminish the pain somewhat, but most dancers suffer extensive second-degree burns across their back, upper arms, and shoulders. The skin will sometimes blister and peel off during the dance; otherwise, it sloughs off in a day or two. Dancers generally spend the first ten days after their ordeal convalescing; after three or four weeks they have healed.

Edward Schieffelin (1976:223) details in his ethnography of the Kaluli the ways in which the gisaro can be understood as the dramatic embodiment and crystallization of the major premises on which their culture is built. Gisaro is a way for them to understand and express their view of the world; the loss and sorrow contained within it, their link with those now invisible to them. He concludes, " the Kaluli [feel] that the forces of growth and life are generated in oppositions, and it is with this, as a life condition, with all its beauty, exuberance, tragedy, and violence, that they try to come to terms in Gisaro."

REFERENCES

FELD, S,
   1990   *Sound and Sentiment.*
           Philadelphia: University of
           Pennsylvania Press

SCHIEFFELIN, B.B.
   1990   *The Give and Take of*
           Everyday Life.
           Cambridge: Cambridge
           University Press.

SCHIEFFELIN, E.L.
   1976   *The Sorrow of the Lonely*
           and the Burning of the
           Dancers. New York: St.
           Martin's Press.

§ THE BEGINNING

Ugatame designed the universe and is of two natures, male and female, like the sun and the moon are two. Sun is light and warm and like a ball of fire. Moon is cool like the light of a firefly. But the sun and the moon are not Ugatame; they are proof that there is Ugatame.

The world is a flat slab of stone, covered with earth, and edged all around with water. There is nothing below it; it goes down as far as there is to go. No dark world beneath the real world exists. Above the world is a bowl turned upside down, and this blue bowl is the sky. The sun begins cupped under the bowl at its eastern lip. It moves through the day to the western edge. As evening comes, the sun slips under the western lip of the blue bowl, and all through the night travels above the curve of the bowl. At last it slides underneath the eastern edge, and it is morning. As the sun moves above the outer convexity of the bowl tiny breaches in the bowl allow pinpoints of light to seep through; these are the stars.

Above the bowl is another world, and it may look like this one. It is Ugatame's home.

INTRODUCTION AND HISTORY

The western half of the island of the main island of New Guinea was originally colonized by the Dutch. In 1969 it came under the jurisdiction of Indonesia, and it is now Irian Jaya. The central highlands of West Irian is rugged, with mountains whose peaks may soar to 4000 meters, and deep valleys below. Three large lakes act as reservoirs and flow south to the Indian Ocean. Of the five vegetational zones, tropical rainforest predominates, with a variety of beeches and oaks. The undergrowth bears ferns and pandanus. Higher altitudes are covered with stunted Alpine growth; valley bottoms are swampy and covered with reeds. It is among these mountains that the 100,000 Kapauku make their home.

Their tribe was named Kapauku by the people to the south; their neighbors to the north call them Ekari. They call themselves "Me"--"the people."

The south coast of New Guinea was linked to the interior by an important intertribal trade network. Since this ran directly through the Kapauku's region, they had extensive contact with both people and goods from beyond the borders of their own territory. However, their mountain ranges, swamps, and extensive rain forests insured their isolation from Western influence until 1938, when the Dutch government stationed officers at an outpost they created near one of the large lakes. This initial contact was brief. The Japanese attack in the southwestern Pacific resulted in the abandonment of this post, and it was not reestablished for nearly ten years. When a new outpost was established, Christian missionaries arrived, their goal being "to see to the spiritual welfare of the people." (Pospisil 1963:3)

KAPAUKU ECONOMY: THE "PRIMITIVE CAPITALISTS"

The Kapauku Papuans are often cited as the prime example of a "simple" society with an egalitarian redistributive system which nevertheless boasts features typical of contemporary capitalist orientation. (Harris 1988; Nanda 1991) In fact, Leopold Pospisil, the leading authority on the Kapauku, labels their economy as "primitive capitalism," characterized by the pursuit of wealth in the form of cowrie shell money, status distinctions based on such wealth, and an ethic of individualism.

Subsistence

Large game is absent in this environment, relegating hunting and trapping to small importance among the Kapauku. There is a paucity too of small game animals; the lakes offer no edible fish. While hunting provides distraction as sport, it is the gathering of crayfish, insects, frogs, rats, and bats which provides important supplements to the daily diet. (It is also a crucial part of the Kapauku economy in that it supplies the raw materials for construction and manufacturing.)

Kapauku subsistence is dependent on two items: sweet potatoes, the staple of the native diet, and pigs.

The Kamu Valley's two very different types of terrain demand the use of two kinds of cultivation, and each household will usually maintain some of each type of garden. Shifting cultivation, with areas cleared by burning, planted with sweet potatoes, and harvested daily, is employed in the mountainous areas. Extensive gardens on the rocky slopes are laboriously fenced off to protect them from wild boars and hungry domesticated pigs, and left to fallow when the plot is exhausted.

The valley is exploited more intensively, employing two methods of rotating crops of sweet potatoes, sugar cane, taro, bananas, cucumbers, gourds, and beans . In all garden types, it is the sweet potato that assumes primacy, with ninety percent of all land devoted to its production.

The domesticated pig plays a role in Kapauku society which can scarcely be overestimated, and which is intricately tied up with other fundamental aspects of Kapauku life and culture.

Pospisil explains that the sweet potato and the pig can be separated neither from one another, nor from the essence of Kapauku economy. Both people and pigs are fed on sweet potatoes. It is the sale of pigs (and pork) which contributes the largest portion of the individual Kapauku's income. And since fat, healthy, fertile pigs depend on the plentiful harvest of sweet potatoes the two are economically bound together. Each is food and each is wealth-- and wealth is the driving force behind Kapauku society. Pospisil reports that "the highest prestige in this society and the highest status of political and legal leadership are achieved not through heritage, bravery in warfare, or knowledge and achievements in religious ceremonialism, but through accumulation and redistribution of capital." (1963:5)

Capital is amassed in the form of shell money, and successful pig breeding is the means to acquire it. So, indirectly, sweet potatoes not only feed human and animal alike, but also provide a way to achieve political power. By providing a way to achieve great wealth--and it is only a wealthy man who rises to leadership and authority--the pig and the sweet potato are joined in "a pivotal role in the wealth-oriented Kapauku society.

Manufacture

Kapauku's limited scope in manufacturing provides contrast to their agriculture sophistication. It is, for the most part, not specialized. Manufactured tools include flint chips, stone axes and knives, and grinding stones. Women's aprons are fashioned from woven tree bark, which is also employed in creating decorative necklaces and armbands worn by both women and men. Knives, used both for surgery and the carving of pork are made of bamboo splinters which break off during the construction of water and insect containers. Rat teeth and bird claws provide raw material to create other carving tools. Agricultural tools, needed for digging, planting, and harvesting are generally made of wood.

Bows and arrows are the first line of weaponry, although mostly used for killing small game, and not in combat. Enemies (and any large game available) are more likely to be challenged with projectiles tipped with long sharp bamboo blades.

While these manufactured tools and weapons are strictly utilitarian in design, the Kapauku demonstrate great artistic skill in their manufacture of net bags, used for both practical and decorative purposes. (Pospisil 1963) They are woven in intricate designs made of string spun from soft inner bark, and often decorated with colored orchid stems. Large nets for fishing and roomy carrying bags are woven by women; the smaller decorative bags worn around the neck or on the shoulder for adornment or used to carry

money are festooned with bright feathers and shells, and are manufactured by men.

Settlement

A Kapauku village typically houses about 120 people and is a scattered arrangement of about fifteen houses. These vary in size, and are constructed of upright planks thatched with reeds or pandanus leaves. This vegetation is also used as insulation between plank layers, with large strips of bark providing the flooring. Each room has a fire, built beneath a chink in the joining of the walls and roof, left expressly for smoke to escape.

Large houses are elevated, leaving a space beneath the structure which houses domesticated pigs. The planking used for walls is also used to build a partition, which runs across the width of the building, dividing it in two. The front section houses the men and adolescent boys in a communal dormitory. The back half is further divided into individual "apartments", one for each married woman and her children.

Some households outgrow this traditional arrangement. If the back section has insufficient room for the number of wives and children, small shelters near the main house are built for each unprovisioned woman and her children.

Money

Reminiscent of the contrast between elaborate techniques of cultivation and simple technology of manufacture, Pospisil (1963) also draws attention to the unusual juxtaposition of "one of the world's most primitive technologies" with what he describes as a "sophisticated and complex" economy. (p. 18).

Kapauku economy rests on the use of money. Cowrie shells and two types of necklaces are used both as money for purchase and exchange and as a measure of value and worth. Both of these types of money can be used to buy food, crops, animals, land, and can purchase cultivation labor, medical care, and magical skills. If one is without money, one is without both respect and social standing. It is only money that affords access to what is important: marriage, social status, livelihood, and personal relationships.

Shells and glass beads, the units of worth, are arranged into denominations, and since they are not locally produced must be secured through trade with peoples living in the coastal lowlands.

Although there is generally an established "customary" or "ideal" price for goods and services, there is also considerable fluctuation which follows the rubric of supply and demand. In addition, prices often reflect the relationship between the individuals involved in the transaction. Often prices are lowered between close relatives, or in dealings with someone whose favor is likely to be valuable in the future or has been depended on in the past.

As would be expected since they are close by, most buying and selling occurs between close relatives, members of local patrilineal kin groups. Barter--that is, exchanging commodities rather than money--has been reduced to a fairly insignificant position among Kapauku, while money payment is mandated for favors and behaviors that in other economic systems would not involve such a transfer. For example, the expression of grief over the death of ones relative must be paid for in money. And there is rarely a crime committed that cannot be erased through adequate shell money payment.

Perhaps the most elaborate rules of sale are constructed for pigs, which is not surprising given their importance in Kapauku culture. In fact, it is the ceremonial pig feast that is the occasion of most active business transactions. Salt is another important item of sale.

In addition to outright buying and selling, the extension of credit has been elaborated (perhaps beyond that of Western economies) as a means of redistributing money. Since there is no mechanism of giving an outright gift, loans assume an important role in establishing oneself as generous and prestigious. "Interest" on a loan is informal, and may be promised by the borrower rather than demanded by the lender. While there is no legal recourse if this promise isn't kept, it carries with it the social sanction of dishonesty, and the likelihood that there will be no further extension of credit in the future.

Pospisil (1963) recounts a story explicating the extent to which the Kapauku "profit motive" has extended to their interactions with Christian missionaries on the island. A missionary church was established, and enjoyed popularity among villagers, who, after Sunday services, received tobacco and other desired goods. Feeling as if his efforts towards their conversion were close to fruition, the missionary grew puzzled as attendance at services began to drop off dramatically over a several week period during which he was waiting for his supplies of goods to be replenished. Once they were finally gone, so were all the attendees at his church. He went to the village to inquire about this distressing turn of events, and was told in no uncertain terms: "No tobacco, no hallelujah." (p. 94)

SOCIAL ORGANIZATION

Kinship and Descent

Each Kapauku can place other people in one of three groups: close friends and kin; acquaintances and strangers; and enemies.

One can trust only those in the first category. Close friends and relatives are the people who offer financial, economic, political and emotional support.

The second classification merges together individuals who are only casual acquaintances with those who are completely unknown. It is worth remembering that since "every stranger is a potential customer" (Pospisil 1963:34) and therefore a potential source of increased wealth, strangers are usually treated with courtesy.

The category of enemy does not necessarily imply personal enmity on an individual's part. Rather, they are defined more by group membership than any hostile interaction. An enemy is someone who belongs to a group which has traditionally had warlike relations with ones father's group.

Although Kapauku reckon descent along both maternal and paternal lines, villages are patrilineal and exogamous, and generally patrilocal. The sib, which is the kinship group of most importance, is a totemic, patrilineal (ideally exogamous) group whose members reckon their descent from a common apical ancestor. The diffuseness of the Kapauku patrilineage renders it of little use for political purposes, limiting its focus to the regulation of marriage and the construction of personal and economic obligatory relationships.

Most day-to-day rights and obligations are incurred within the localized patrilineal group; it is members of this group that an individual will depend upon for amassing bride-price or gathering allies in times of conflict with outsiders. Larger political amalgamations (confederations) are established through kinship ties, forged by marriages, with other lineages.

Marriage

The arrangement of a marriage ideally occurs between the families of the prospective groom and brothers and mother of the prospective bride. Collecting a high bride-price takes precedence over the preferences expressed by the woman to be married. However, mothers may set a bride-price they know cannot be met expressly for the purpose of discouraging an undesirable prospect

Elopements are not infrequent, despite the fact that they are considered improper. When this occurs, it is set right b y negotiating a bride-price after the fact, indicating that families of the eloping couple have accepted the union The pig feast, an occasion for men and women of marriageable age from neighboring villages to come together, is a primary opportunity for courtship. Premarital sex is generally not punished, although it is frowned upon for its potential to diminish a woman's bride-price. Premarital pregnancy,

however, is a much more seriously disapproved matter.

When divorce occurs, the bride-price must be returned, which is a serious consequence. (Divorce--usually occurring because a woman has left her husband-- is, in fact, cited as a common instigator of warfare.) In such an instance, small children generally remain with their mother, and when they reach the age of about seven, are likely to join their father's village. Unless advanced age or illness prevents it, a widow is expected to remarry within a reasonable amount of time after her husband's death.

One reason polygyny is widely practiced is that it provides an opportunity for men to gain status. The acquisition of multiple wives, granting status because it is an indicator of the husband's ability to pay multiple bride-prices, is a display of wealth among the Kapauku much in the same way the acquisition of expensive jewelry and other luxury items is in the United States.

However, while polygyny is an ideal for which Kapauku men will strive, it is an expensive venture and not easily attained. (About one-third of all marriages are polygynous.) As we have seen, Kapauku economy depends largely on plant cultivation and pig husbandry. While it is the agricultural activities that provide most of the food, it is through pigs that men achieve status, power and authority. If a husband can afford multiple wives, they will ultimately help him earn more money and prestige through their tending of pigs and sweet potatoes.

Family and household

Household composition varies somewhat. It always consists, minimally, of a nuclear family, but usually also includes other consanguineal or affinal kin. In addition to being the basic Kapauku unit of residence it is also, to a large extent, the basic unit of production and consumption.

Whoever owns the house is considered the "head" within the household; he is responsible for organizing production and harvesting activities, because he is ultimately responsible for assuring that household members are adequately fed. He is also charged with maintaining harmony and cooperation among the other men, which must be accomplished by setting an example, and through his own personal skills of persuasion. Despite owning the house he has no formal recourse for enforcing his wishes. He must also be careful not to overstep certain boundaries in exercising control over the members of other nuclear families living within the household.

POLITICAL ORGANIZATION

Authority and leadership in the setting of a family (nuclear or polygynous) or an individual household is well defined among the Kapauku. It may be based on ownership; it may be based on kinship. Authority and leadership on a larger level is not formally defined in this way.

Positions of leadership in Kapauku society are held exclusively by men, who appropriate the products of women's labor in order to play their political games. "...Male dominance is by no means characteristic of all human societies. Rather, as in the Kapauku case, it arises only under particular sets of circumstances, which, if changed, will alter the way in which men and women relate to one another." (Havilland 1990:39)

That men are in formal positions of leadership must be viewed in the context of the entire fabric of Kapauku society, however. Pospisil (1963) points out that, despite whatever "ideal" may be espoused formally, one must not overlook the reality that, in many instances, "the father and husband is only a figurehead, while the actual power rests with his wife. " (p. 42) He says of one such woman, with whom he was negotiating a purchase of pork, "despite the fact that she is the individual who makes the important decisions in the family, she never forgets the conventions of Kapauku culture." (p 42)

Found in many societies throughout Melanesia and New Guinea is a person in a position of leadership called the "big man." It is through personal attributes and achievements that such stature is achieved. Big man status is neither inherited nor elected. As a result of public behaviors-- generosity chief among them--and great wealth which facilitates such behavior, a man sets himself apart from others in the community, attracting loyal followers. As he continues to amass wealth, so too he gathers his reputation. He sponsors feasts, helps young men gather bridewealth, and by so doing engenders the obligation of those whom he has helped.

Among the Kapauku there is such a big man role. It is called tonowi, which means "rich one."

The tonowi

The Kapauku tonowi embodies the typical traits of the characteristic big man. His position is an informal one; he sets himself apart from his fellows with his wealth, his generosity, and his verbal skills. Often he may have proven to be brave in war, or well-versed in shamanism, but these are traits that only enhance his power; they are not essential to be a tonowi.

A tonowi does not have the formal authority to enforce his will. He offers his suggestions, makes his wishes known, and encourages people to accept his decisions. Although his position is an informal one, the tonowi assumes the mantle of leadership on a great number of occasions. It is he who acts as a representative of his own group in their dealings with outsiders and other villages. Within his group he negotiates settlements and judges blame in disputes. It is generally the case that social control among the Kapauku is effected by persuasion rather than by force. Owing to the desirability of amassing a fortune, economic inducements often act as the most effective incentive. Fines or threats of fines are frequently enough to exact conformity.

Given the extreme value Kapauku culture places on wealth, it is hardly surprising that one who has achieved great wealth would be deemed successful and worthy of admiration. When speaking of big man status, however, mere possession of wealth is never enough; not all who are rich are tonowi. The wealth must be generously distributed, and Pospisil notes there may be severe consequences if it is not. "[I]n some regions...selfish and greedy individuals, who have amassed huge personal properties, but who have failed to comply with the Kapauku requirement of "generosity" towards their less fortunate tribesmen may be, and actually frequently are, put to death." (p. 49) Pospisil was, in fact, among the Kapauku at a time when just such an occurrence took place.

Even in those regions where these measures are not taken, wealthy individuals who hoard rather than share their fortunes are shunned, ridiculed, and eventually brought into line, thus ensuring more equitable distribution of capital.

Of course, given the nature of his position and the lack of formal recourse, even a tonowi who is generous and well-respected cannot force others to do what he wishes. This is one instance where his personal charm and verbal gifts become of the utmost importance. If met with resistance, he may become agitated and begin to shout taunts; he makes long eloquent speeches outlining the wisdom of his decision, citing rules that support his position, finally offering threats to solidify his position. In extreme cases, he may begin to perform what is known as "the mad dance", or abruptly stop his ranting and cry piteously about the misconduct in question and the obstinence of the transgressor. Some tonowi are so adept at this performance that they can summon genuine tears, a sight which usually proves moving enough to at last secure the compliance of any unwilling party. (Pospisil 1968) This facet of the role is crucial enough to jeopardize a wealthy man's ability to become a tonowi in its absence. Wealthy and generous individuals who are shy and soft spoken, or who disdain public confrontation, cannot ascend to the position.

The generosity required of a wealthy individual must be expressed in culturally appropriate forms. Since the native economy does not include gift giving, it is through his willingness to make loans that the tonowi acquires his political power. By extending credit to those in need, wealthy men gain both the prestige that accrues from generosity as well as the indebtedness and loyalty of his creditor. The tonowi is then in a good position to have others follow his dictates: those who are already in his debt comply so as not to have repayment of their loan demanded. Those who have not yet asked for an extension of credit comply lest they jeopardize their chance of successful borrowing in the future. Thus the widest possible alliances are forged, and the tonowi exacts loyalty from the majority of the villagers.

Besides those to whom he has extended credit, a tonowi also find support by taking "apprentices" into his household. Since every Kapauku man aspires to riches, a young man seizes the opportunity to join the household of an older, wealthy man. He is lent a pig, is given room and board and the opportunity to benefit from the tonowi's business acumen. If the young man appears to be a promising pupil, his benefactor might allow him to buy a female piglet, in order to begin accumulating his wealth in earnest. The final act of generosity is a loan to make up the brideprice he will need to marry. In return, these apprentices work in the garden and household, and act as bodyguards. They are loyal in the event of a dispute; in war, they offer their lives. Once they are established in their own right, those the tonowi has called "my boys" continue to function as loyal supporters.

A tonowi, much like any Kapauku, also depends upon his close kin for political support . Members of his kin group will follow a tonowi for all the same economic reasons others do, but will additionally acquiesce out of genuine affection.

Since the tonowi's wealth is dependent upon successful pig breeding, it is far from secure. If a tonowi makes a poor management decision, or has a run of bad luck, his fortune may be lost. Because the loss of wealth will result in the loss of tonowi status, Kapauku political structure is rarely static over long periods of time. Pig breeding offers a vehicle for wealth which is accessible to many Kapauku, contributing to the flux in the status system. As one man loses power, another steps in to take his place. The result is a flexible, frequently shifting power structure, with no individual in a position of authority for an extended period of time.

THE CULTURE OF INDIVIDUALISM

Economic individualism

One of the most striking features of Kapauku culture is the overriding emphasis on the individual. Evidence for this orientation as well as its consequences are found throughout their beliefs, behaviors, and institutions.

Pospisil asserts: "All Kapauku economic undertakings are executed primarily because... 'I need,' or 'I want to do it for my own benefit.' I have never heard an economic argument in which the needs of the social group have been put forward as a justification for a position taken by a discussant." (1963:89)

This attention to ones own needs, and the attempt to acquire that which will satisfy them, has resulted in individual ownership of all goods, with practically nothing viewed as communal property. Houses, pigs, land, canoes are all cited as items owned by a single individual. More surprisingly, even large areas of forest are claimed by individual owners. The exception to this is rocky mountainous areas and large streams, which are not claimed by individuals but are rather the property of lineages and sublineages. Pospisil (1963) suggests that fishless

waters and barren, rocky land on which nothing will grow hold no economic interest. Thus, they are not claimed by individuals because no one cares to own something of no economic value. What is valuable, however, are any game animals which may roam around these mountaintops and streams. They, when caught, become the property of the individual trapper, due to the access granted by the lineage ownership.

Upon occasion, two individuals may jointly own a house. When this is the case, however, each individual can identify which sheets of bark and planks of wood are their contribution to the building--and hence their own. Those items which service the village as a whole--for example, fences, bridges, and main ditches--are in fact owned piecemeal by individuals, who claim ownership to particular sections of the structures.

Individualism is the vantage point from which to view all economic cooperation within each household. No single meal served is exempt from individual ownership. Each meal has a host who owns the food. When household residents work in the garden, tend the pigs, dig a ditch, they are entering into an individual contract with the owner of the house, and they will be paid, either in shell money, pork, or other goods. When the work is completed, even if the task was performed by several household members, it is still not viewed in the aggregate as a single large accomplishment with many contributors. In fact, rather than striving for consistency of the overall project when working together, Kapauku will take pains to make their own contribution unique enough that it can be recognized as distinct from the portion done by any other individual. If a fence is to be built, each individual worker builds a section they can remember as their own, refer to as their property, and for which they will be solely responsible. Garden work is divided up such that each individual is only responsible for one discrete section.

Multiple leaders without consensus

The cultural thread of Kapauku individualism can be found running through the institutions of the society. As we have seen, the tonowi--the most important of these political institutions---rises to his position based on individually acquired, and not inherited, wealth. However, great wealth without the assertive and polished personal characteristics is not sufficient for success as a tonowi.

There is also no formal cooperation among the men who achieve tonowi status at the same time. Generally, one man is charged with settling the legal aspects of conflicts and the other with attending to more broadly stated political issues. Conventionally, they do not confer and attempt to reach consensus. Rather, each one considers the facts and renders a judgment independent of the other. If a dispute arises, deciding whose authority takes precedence is simple: the leader who arrives on the scene first is the one who renders judgment. Thus, there is, in Kapauku political and legal organization, no council of elders, or any formal group who deliberates for the benefit of the community as a whole. A tonowi's verdict is presented, and then it is up to him to sway opinion to support it.

Socialization into individualism

Individualism and independence are among the most important lessons in the education of young Kapauku. Often this teaching begins in the all-important setting of the garden. Early on each boy and girl is given a garden or section of a garden to care for on their own. A girl plants, weeds, and harvests her own plot, which is separated from those of her mother and older sisters. This allows her success or failure to be plainly seen on its own merit.

A boy's garden too is an occasion to begin learning the necessary skills that will serve him later on as he aspires to amassing his fortune. The yield of his garden belongs solely to the boy, who enters into financial relationships, as debtor or creditor, with his father and older brothers. To teach him a lesson, a father may purposely cheat his son to see what the child will do.

Pospisil (1963) observed a "lesson" that proved to him the seriousness with which this education is regarded. He recounts that one day, "I heard a loud howling and lamentation coming from one of the houses. When I entered the structure I found to my surprise a middle-aged, muscular man squatting in the middle of the room, crying and yelling while a boy, about eleven years old, was screaming at him and hitting him with a stick. The man was being beaten by his own son. The reason for the excitement was that the father owed his son 2 bomoje shells which he refused to pay back. Thus the boy had a right to punish his debtor. However, by inflicting the beating he abrogated his right to the debt; the father's obligation to repay was annulled After the beating was over and the enraged boy departed, the father wiped away his tears and smiled with great satisfaction: 'My boy will be quite a businessman, but he must learn not to trust anybody.' In addition to the lesson in commerce the whole affair proved to be most satisfactory to the happy father, as he assured me. Not only had he gained 2 cowries, but the beating administered by his son, he insisted, was so painless that he received the wealth for practically nothing." (p. 30)

When children misbehave they are punished, but as a learning tool rather than a tactic to engender enforcement born of fear. Children should ideally view reprimand as a consequence of past behavior. It is not desirable for a child to be "well-behaved" in an unthinking way. Punishment conveys information which the child is expected to use in choosing his or her own course in the future. Likewise, children are asked, and not told, to do things. This too derives from the belief that an individual must be allowed the freedom to choose. The true essence of life is thought to be an unfettered cooperation of the mind and the body.

Without the individual freedom to allow the soul to direct the actions of the body, the soul attempts to leave--resulting in death. Kapauku society has no institutions which limit this individual freedom; there is no slavery, there are no jails, and they never take prisoners of war. Killing, to their way of thinking, is far more humane than incarceration, which would result in a slow death caused by the absence of personal freedom.

Individualism in warfare

Unlike so many of their lowland neighbors, the Kapauku do not relish the idea of war. They regard it as an occasion for the destruction of gardens and pigs, and the loss of loved ones. The economic consequences of such occurrences are dreaded. If a close relative instigates a conflict, one is obliged to help, but not without regret. (And, in fact, the cause of any war can be traced back to one individual engaged in a dispute with another.) In the rare instances when war erupts, fighting follows an individualistic pattern. There is no strategizing among groups of warriors, no attacks planned en masse. In fact, participants spread out so that when an enemy is shot there is no doubt as to the identity of the killer, who is later recognized in a personal victory dance. If several snipers stalk an enemy in his village, only one man is designated to carry out the attack, the others waiting under cover.

RELIGION AND EXPRESSIVE CULTURE

The Kapauku believe that the Ugatame, who dwells beyond the sky, created the universe and has predetermined all the events within it, past, present and future. Spirits of Ugatame's creation frequently appear to Kapauku as shadows in the trees, which make rustling or scraping sounds as evidence. Less often, theses shadows appear in dreams or visions, sometimes in human form. These incarnations can be used by the dreamer as helpers or protectors, for both good or evil purposes. Likewise, the souls of dead kindred can be called upon to provide aid to their living kin.

Science, secularism, and the supernatural

The religious philosophy of the group is intriguing, in that it is not, as Pospisil (1963) puts it, "studded with numerous rationally inexplicable dogmas that are so characteristic of the world's great religions." (p. 92)

The Kapauku hold a rationalistic and logical view of the world that resembles scientific thought. Their outlook on the world is internally consistent, depending upon that which can be perceived through the senses, and follows logically from those perceptions. Once these premises are granted, that which contradicts these expectations is rejected out of hand. Following from this, since the only things that exist are things that can be perceived by the senses, the supernatural does not exist. People believe in it, but it is not real. They are thus none to eager to explain the unknown and speculate on the whys and wherefores of the world's mysteries. When asked to do so, they are most likely to reply, "I don't know," and be satisfied to leave it at that. Ethnographer Pospisil (1963) reports never having witnessed any purely philosophical musings, speculations on the enigmas of life, or arguments focusing solely on the supernatural.

This logical universe is relativistic. Determining "bad" and "good" can only be accomplished in context. Hence, when asked "Is killing a man good or bad?" the reaction is one of both surprise and confusion . After some thought, the answer will be itself a question. "Killing of which man, and good for whom?" (Posposil 1963)

KAPAUKU

Ceremonies

Kapauku ceremonies stand in contrast to the elaborate rituals found in the lowlands. Unlike ceremonial events which typically focus on religion and the supernatural, and are often communal in nature, Kapauku ceremonies appear both secular and individualistic. All have an "owner" who is individually responsible for their outcome and who will personally gain prestige if it is successful.

The lack of preoccupation with the supernatural is reflected in the fact that Kapauku ceremonial life revolves primarily around the realm of economics. Any elements one might deem "magical" are very minor portions of ceremonial events such as weddings, births, or feasts. Certainly the magical acts are not considered essential: tonowi sponsoring feasts assert that the success of an event is due solely to their own labor, and not to any supernatural guidance.

Absent from Kapauku culture are artistic renderings of supernatural beings, fertility rites, elaborate mortuary customs, and group initiation ceremonies. The most elaborate ceremonial production, the pig feast, is not religious in nature, but is designed to gain wealth and display status. Performers in the ceremonies are not attempting to influence the supernatural to send good fortune their way; they expect direct economic benefit as a result of their participation.

Pig feasts

The most important Kapauku ceremony, and certainly one which is economic in focus, is the pig feast, which is a cycle of events lasting several months.

It is instigated by a tonowi's decision to host the feast. Here, he can sell pork for shell money, give away pork to gain prestige, and establish his primacy over other rich men who may aspire to his position. The construction of a dance house and feasting houses are then begun, and these endeavors have a series of rituals associated with them. Following their construction, there is a three month period of nightly dances, attended by nearby villagers. Special songs are composed for singing in the dance houses during these months, and are regarded as the valuable personal property of the single individual who composed them.

There are actually several grand feasts before the final one. Dancing, singing, and courtship is ongoing. By the time the culminating feast is held, there have been perhaps two thousand guests and several hundred pigs slaughtered and distributed. Profits in shell money may be enormous. Great feasts are talked about for years after their occurrence.

Illness, curing, and death

Illness is sent by spirits or sorcerers, and cured by shamans, who often are helped by spirits of their own. A shaman's curative armamentarium includes spells and prayers, treatments made from medicinal and magical plants, ritual washings of the ailing individual, and the removal of foreign objects from a victim's body. Shamans also have the power of preventive medicine, should an individual be aware of a sorcerer's evil attempt and wish to forestall the anticipated illness.

Both shamans--whose magic is used towards positive ends--and sorcerers--whose gifts are essentially evil-- can acquire their status through such spiritual or dreaming visitations. Women and men who are shamans practice preventive magic and curative ceremonies. Those who are sorcerers can send illness, economic ruin, or death .

Certain older women, whose souls have been eaten by flesh-hungry spirits, and replaced by the spirit's evil presence while they sleep, appear ordinary by day. But during the night she pursues all the corpses who have been former victims of the evil spirit now residing within her soul, and consumes what is left of the corpses' flesh. Punishment of these ghouls does not include death, which action would only release the spirit possessing her, sending it in search of a new home. Instead, since ghouls are believed to be so possessed due to the black magic of a sorcerer, the individual sorcerer deemed responsible is sought out and killed, thus effectively ending the ghoul's ordeal.

Death is invariably attributed to spirits or sorcerers, no matter what its outward cause. The soul, once departing the body, will spend the day among the forests, but comes home to the village at nightfall, in case kin-group members need help or seek vengeance. Days spent by departed souls in the forest is the totality of the Kapaukun "afterworld" beliefs; there is no sense that there is another dwelling place for the dead after life in the village. Given the expectations of the Kapauku that the souls of the dead may act in their behalf, it is not surprising that great care is taken with burial practices to achieve this end. While the torso of the dead is buried, the head is left above ground, sheltered from the elements by a web of branches, with enough open space between them to provide a window.

A world of quantity

As an outgrowth of their emphasis on objectivity, profit, and exactness, Kapauku are oriented to a world where the quantitative holds sway over the qualitative. They have outstanding mathematical abilities and a highly elaborate counting system, both valuable skills in their money economy. They value high numbers and large volume. When shown pictures in an American magazine, they directed most of their attention to counting the number of teeth in a smile, windows in office buildings, cars on the street, and, with most enthusiasm, the huge number of spectators in the crowd at a football game.

Pospisil (1963) found that informants gained great pleasure in being able to count the thousands of glass beads he used as money. After many hours spent counting, he would be told: "You have 6722 beads in your boxes. That means you have spent 623 beads since Gubeeni counted your money three days ago." (p. 94) He

reflects on this with the admission that his finances were never so much in order as during his times in the field among the Kapauku.

He too benefited from their understanding of his work back home. After giving the villagers a "lecture" on agriculture, he in turn was handed several chickens, with the explanation that they remembered that he was always paid to lecture to his anthropology students in the United States. (Muller 1990)

REFERENCES

MULLER, K.
1990   *Spice Islands: Exotic Eastern Indonesia.* Lincolnwood: Passport Books.

POSPISIL, L.
1963   *The Kapauku Papuans of West New Guinea.* New York: Holt, Rinehart and Winston.

§ THE BEGINNING

In the world there is life. Why did death come to the world?

"When the moon died, it returned to life again, to pass again across the sky. 'Everyone will do as I do,' said the moon. When a person has died, don't think that he will just die and lie there.... Take heed, follow what I, the moon do: I die and then live again, and die again only to live again. Everyone should do as I do.'

But the hare contradicted the moon. 'No!' he said. 'A person is born and he must die also...'

The moon argued with him, and said, 'Watch me. I'm going to die and then I'll come alive again. Watch me and learn, and then we can both do it.' But the hare refused. So the moon split his mouth open. The hare became the split-mouth hare that people chase.

The moon and the hare argued with each other, and harangued each other. The moon said, 'Take my advice...a person will die and yet return!' But the hare refused, so the moon took a hatchet and split his mouth. Then the hare scratched the moon's face! That's why you can still see marks on the moon's face, because the hare scratched it and the scratches festered. When the hare had spoiled the moon's face, the two of them separated. They spent the next day separate, and the day after that. That's how their anger rose and they fought, chopping each others' mouths and clawing each other's faces." (Biesele 1976:321-322)

INTRODUCTION AND HISTORY

The San are a hunting and gathering people living in Southern Africa. Their nearest neighbors are a herding group, the Khoi, with whom they shared for centuries most of southern Africa west of the Eastern Cape. San are a varied people in terms of looks and language, and include people living in Angola, Botswana, Zambia and Namibia.

In pre-colonial times, San population was estimated at up to 300,000. However, the arrival of the Dutch in the mid-1650s resulted in the near-decimation of the San people. By the 1850s, Dutch expansion and settlement caused conflict between the groups, escalating into bitter warfare. Systematic genocide of the San by the Dutch led many to fear for their survival as a people.

The group who has been studied most extensively is the !Kung San of the Dobe area, who are by now most likely the most thoroughly documented foraging society in the world. (Lee 1984)

The Dobe Region

The Dobe area is situated in the northwest portion of the Kalahari desert, and has been home to hunters and gatherers for thousands of years. It is a grouping of ten waterholes, arranged in three sections. To the north along a dry riverbed is a peculiar outcropping of granite and limestone with a large foragable area . In the south is one major waterhole with several smaller seasonal watering places scattered around it. The center region contains the Aha Hills, made up of several low ranges. This area lacks surface water and thus contains no permanent settlements. These three regions taken together span an area of about 3000 square miles.

Several hundred years ago, San developed trading relationships with peoples to the east. In the late nineteenth century Tswana cattle herders came to the Dobe during the summer rainy season to graze their cattle, hunt, and trade. Tswana relied on San as trackers and butchers, helping to transport the game back to the east when the summer rains ended. It was at about this time that European hunters too came to the Dobe region to secure furs and ivory.

Within the Dobe region currently, the largest group of non-San are the Herero peoples, pastoralists with thousands of head of cattle in their herds.

Access to water is a problem in the northern part of the Kalahari, and permanent waterholes are not sufficient for the San's needs. They depend too on seasonal waterholes, depressions between the dunes that fill after heavy rains. Some are small and hold water for only a few weeks; others are up to 300 feet long, holding water for months on end. A small source of water is that which can be found in the hollow interior of some trees; in an emergency, there are roots which can be dug up and their moisture extracted. The San plan their movement around these changing sources of water, spending the rainy summer months near the seasonal waterholes, and the wintertime close to the permanent sources.

Plentiful and varied game provide the San with good hunting. They can name over 250 animal species available to them in their environment. Warthog, wildebeest, giraffe, antelope, and other hooved mammals are the most abundant game. Although lions, leopards, and cheetahs are hunting in the same environment, !Kung appear not to be fearful of them. They sleep out in the open, even without protective fires, and do not consider themselves in jeopardy.

There are also more than one hundred species of birds in the Dobe area, which are hunted for food. Of particular value is the ostrich, whose shells, once the eggs are eaten, can be washed and used for water containers. Reptiles and amphibians are present too, but there are no fish. Insects, while not a part of the diet, provide poison for arrow tips.

The !Kung divide the year into five seasons, characterized by differing patterns of rainfall. Although there is a general pattern to the precipitation--rain predominates in the hot summer months, and is scarce in the winter--there is considerable yearly variation, resulting in great unpredictability. Consequently, they must be continually adaptive, prepared to accommodate high-rainfall years, low-rainfall years, and extensive variation from region to region.

!KUNG SAN

Settlement

A !Kung encampment consists of grass huts arranged roughly in a circle, constructed around an area of clearing in the center. Since mobility is the hallmark of !Kung life, these huts are constructed quickly and rarely used for more than a few months at a time. Camps are located near water holes, and the conventional area that a group exploits is one which can be accomplished in a day's walk, round-trip, in any direction. The !Kung houses reflect the season in which they are built. During the dry season, sites are located near dependable sources of water. Huts built for use during the rainy season are constructed with thickly thatched roofs to provide shelter from the punishing rains. During times of year with less extreme weather, camp is often set up without building shelter of any kind. A fire may be built, the group sleeps, and the next day moves on.

In addition to huts, other structures are erected to store belongings to keep them both of sight and out of reach: arrow poison must not be accessible to children, and dried strips of meat must be kept away from the dogs.

Characteristic of traditional camp construction was the circular arrangement of huts or sleeping position: the !Kung faced one another. In more recent days, as cattle have become important, some encampments are not only more permanent, they are oriented with the hut doorway facing the cattle compound, rather than another hut.

SUBSISTENCE

The foraging !Kung can provide for themselves a bountiful and varied diet. Plant foods are plentiful and nutritious, and make up the majority of their diet. Women have an intricate and complex knowledge of their plant environment, distinguishing more than a hundred varieties of edible plants from those which are poisonous or otherwise undesirable. A single gathering foray can result in fifty pounds of food, easily enough for ten days' sustenance. Most important in their diet is the mongongo, a protein-rich nut found abundantly on trees near every waterhole. In addition to its high nutritional value and availability, mongongo nuts are also easily stored and not often affected by seasonal or environmental variation.

A simple digging stick is the only tool required for gathering, sufficient for digging up roots and tubers, as well as ferreting out burrowing mammals. It can also be used as a carrying pole, slung across the shoulder with the load tied on.

Transporting the food that has been gathered requires more elaboration. A large suede cape, called a kaross, provides the most useful means for carrying both food and firewood, by forming a sturdy pouch close to the body. Because it is worn close to the body, it is very efficient for heavy loads. Children too are carried in the kaross, which also doubles as a blanket at night. Leather pouches, net bags, and infant slings are among the other carrying devices so important to the !Kung, who rely on containers that can allow them ease of mobility while carrying hundreds of small food items daily

The !Kung follow a very specific pattern in their exploitation of the environment. Richard Lee, an ethnographer who has studied the group extensively, says bluntly, "the !Kung typically occupy a campsite for a period of weeks and eat their way out of it." (1984:44) They do this by venturing out from the campsite in increasing rings, walking further each day to find food. Gathering is done in two ways: some people stay closer to camp and gather all edibles they can; others venture farther afield looking for those things that are particularly appealing. (This leads to longer walking distances each day, as closer supplies are used up.) By pooling their resources at the end of the day, all people have not only enough, they also have a variety.

Although hunting provides a minor portion of the !Kung diet (roughly thirty percent), meat is nonetheless a valuable commodity. While its scarcity may explain its value, it has been suggested (Lee 1984) that the sociability it occasions may be of even greater importance. Meat provides more than protein; it also provides social opportunity. The killing of a large animal is followed by a commensurately large feast, enjoyed by all. Distribution of cooked meat is an arduous affair; it is portioned and reapportioned until everyone has received the amount deemed satisfactory.

Bows and arrows, spears, knives, and ropes are the most reliable tools for hunting. Dogs can be useful, especially in cornering prey and keeping it at bay until it can be speared. Animals need not be out in the open to be fair game. Many are pursued in their burrows, using a special tool equipped with a hooked end for just this purpose. Older hunters with less agility rely on snares to net unsuspecting hare, guinea fowl, and small antelope.

Essential in successful hunting of this sort are refined tracking skills, possessed amply by the !Kung. Not only can a hunter tell what sort of animal has made a track, and how many have passed by; they can also determine its sex, age, health, diet, as well as speed and time of travel. For example, the placement of tracks in relation to trees indicate whether the animal was seeking shade from afternoon sun; the amount of sand or twigs in the depression of a hoofprint can indicate how long ago it was made.

EGALITARIANISM

Despite the !Kung appreciation for meat, displays of enthusiasm for a successful hunt--and successful hunter-- are tempered by the importance, in !Kung society, of maintaining egalitarianism, which necessitates the avoidance of undue praise for an individual and that person's accomplishments. As Lee (1984:49-50) explains: "Insulting the meat is one of the central practices of the !Kung that serves to maintain egalitarianism. Even though some men are better hunters than others, their behavior is molded by the group to minimize the tendency toward self-praise

and to channel their energies into socially beneficial activities. As a result, the existence of differences in hunting prowess does not lead to a system of Big Men in which a few talented individuals tower over the others in terms of prestige."

In a story that has become perhaps the most widely cited example of this practice, Lee tells of how he learned this lesson, after mistakenly calling attention to his own largesse, despite his best of intentions. His accurate study of the subsistence economy of the !Kung mandated that he not interfere with their food procurement in any way. Thus, Lee gave !Kung only tobacco and medical supplies in return for their time and talk. His own large supply of canned goods seemed, to him, a glaring inequity in the face of the !Kung larder, which was empty by the end of the day.

As he prepared to leave the Kalahari, Lee was determined to provide, as a going-away feast, an ox of such grand proportions that it would provide at least four pounds of meat for every man, woman, and child in attendance. Satisfied that he had found such an animal, Lee was very pleased with himself indeed.

It was not long before word of the purchase began to spread, and people began to approach him for confirmation of the rumor. Lee was only too pleased to confirm that he had, in fact, purchased a large and well-known animal from a neighboring group, and was indeed planning to slaughter and serve it to the !Kung. He waited for the delight and gratitude he felt he surely deserved, but was taken aback by the reaction with which he was met instead. One by one, individuals approached him to offer nothing but chastisement for the pitiful specimen he intended to serve. A close friend implored him to explain his stinginess: "What has happened to change your heart? That sack of guts and bones ...will hardly feed one camp...Perhaps you have forgotten that we are not few, but many. Or are you too blind to tell the difference between a proper cow and an old wreck? That ox is thin to the point of death."

Lee was demoralized, and day after day, as the feast drew nearer, was warned that of course he must serve the beast, since it was already paid for, but not to expect much of a festive evening to follow, given the sorry offering which would surely send people home hungry. The feast came and went, and indeed the ox was fat, and served the people for 2 days and nights of revelry. But all the while the !Kung were eating they were proclaiming their disdain for the thin, wretched ox. Realizing that he had been fooled, but not sure why, Lee pursued the matter. Finally he was told that the people had been acting in their characteristic manner, the way in which all hunters are treated despite the bounty they might bring home. An informant explained, "Yes, when a young man kills much meat he comes to think of himself as a chief or a big man, and he thinks of the rest of us as his servants or inferiors. We can't accept this. We refuse one who boasts, for someday his pride will make him kill somebody. So we always speak of his meat as worthless. This way we cool his heart and make him gentle." (1979:156)

SOCIAL ORGANIZATION

!Kung "camps" or bands are the traditional form of !Kung organization. They usually contain between ten and thirty members who live and move together for the majority of the year. While membership is flexible, it is not random. Individuals are kin to one another, and it is a core of related elders around whom the band is centered.

These older, central group members are generally thought of as the people to whom the resources "belong." However, their role is more as guardian or host of the land and water than one who has formal ownership, since there is no individual ownership of property among the !Kung. When encampments are established around a waterhole, the land that surrounds it and the bounty contained therein is owned by a kin group. While permission must be asked of the elders in order to avail oneself

of the resources, it is rarely refused. The older members of the camp or band have simply been associated with the resources longest, so it follows that theirs would be the strongest ties. Women and men who function in this capacity also provide the basis for the kinship ties that create the group. The original central members are siblings, who bring their spouses into the group. Their children and their spouses are added as the years go on, with no tradition of unilocality. Both men and women function equally as core elders of the group.

Relations among these groups are maintained in balance by reciprocal visiting. Acquiring rights to territories is accomplished through birth (one has rights to parents' territory) and also through marriage (through which there is claim to the spouse's territory). Additionally, visiting between siblings and in-laws acquired through one's childrens' marriages extend an individual's rightful territory.

Kinship

The flexibility of the !Kung living arrangement is the key to its success. Membership of the group changes often. Yet flexibility must still have something beneath to give it stability. Among the !Kung that is provided by kinship ties.

The band is, at base, a "unit of sharing," which demands peace and cooperation among its members. (Lee 1984: 61) It must also be balanced in terms of numbers of productive adults who can provide food and labor, and young, dependent members who cannot. Thus, the composition of the group will change as patience wears thin; it will also shift as the number of children becomes too large to support, or too small to ensure a future.

When arguments escalate to the point at which they may jeopardize the cooperation and harmony of the group, the !Kung penchant for going off and visiting kin in another group functions as a sort of "safety valve." Lee (1984) observes that it is more often the depletion of patience than the depletion of food resources in an area that causes some to move on and regroup

The !Kung system of kinship is extremely complex, and presented quite a challenge to ethnographers attempting to understand both how people reckoned their connections to one another, and also the functions served by their associations.

All kinship relations among the !Kung are of one of two types, either "joking" or playful relationships, or "avoidance" relationship, based on "fear" or, more accurately, respect. Ones actions with a joking relative are characterized by comfort, relaxation, and familiarity. With some (for example, grandparents) there is a great display of affection. With others (such as peers, and especially those of the opposite sex) there may be an element of flirtation, and even outright bawdiness. However, with avoidance relatives, manners are refined and more aloof. The relationship between parents and children falls into this category, demonstrating the authority parents have over their children, and the respect children are expected to show their parents. Parents-in-law and children-in-law are also avoidance relatives, and it is the mother-in-law/son-in-law and father-in-law/daughter-in-law relationships that are the most severely constrained. While custom forbids conversation between them, in practice they usually do speak to one another. (Lee 1984)

One unique feature of the system is the relationships forged by special naming practices. There are very few names found among the !Kung, because children are supposed to be given names of their ancestors. Since everyone must be named for someone, many people have the same name. !Kung have only a single name (not a "first" and "last" name), and thus rely on nicknames to identify individuals. The sharing of a name with someone else engenders a special kinship relation with that person, carrying with it a host of other connections, all based on the coincidental sharing of the same name. Thus, for example, a woman married to a man with a particular name calls any man with that name "husband." If your mother's name is the same as another person's mother,

you and that person are siblings--because you are children of the "same" mother.

These relationships forged by naming have a direct impact on marriage rules: one may not marry a person with the same name as one's parent or sibling. If you are a woman whose father has a common name, and in addition, have several brothers with common names as well, fully half the population may be eliminated as marriage partners solely on the basis of their names.

Marriage

Traditionally, marriages are arranged for children by their parents, who begin to contemplate their children's marriage partners soon after the baby is born. Parents whose children are betrothed to each other in early childhood may exchange gifts for ten years or more before it is time for the children to wed.

There is a rigid system of rules guiding the universe that defines an appropriate marriage partner. Incest taboos extend beyond parents and siblings to what we would term first and second cousins, as well as aunts, uncles, nieces and nephews. Beyond these proscriptions based on ties of blood and naming, individuals belonging to the avoidance categories of kin are likewise eliminated. This severely restricts the number of potential spouses.

Once the proper kinship and name relationship has been settled, there are personal characteristics that parents also consider necessary in a marital partner for their child. Parents are especially cautious in choosing sons-in-law, who must be good hunters, not given to fighting, and belong to a friendly family who enjoy participating in exchange. To this end, couples may begin their lives together in adolescence, with the chosen boy coming to live with the "bride's" family for as much as a decade, hunting for them and remaining under close scrutiny.

!Kung marriages sometimes have a stormy beginning, presumably due to the tradition of a "marriage-by-capture" ceremony, in which the bride is forcibly removed from her hut and presented to her groom. Since all first marriages are arranged by parents, the couple involved have had no say in choosing a partner. Girls who are very displeased with their parents' selection may protest violently--often kicking and screaming during "capture" and running away at the conclusion of the ceremony--which can sometimes result in the dissolution of the arrangement. Even if the protests are ignored and eventually stop, Lee (1984:79) suggests that this behavior is "eloquent testimony to the independence of !Kung women from both parents and husbands." In fact, more than half of all !Kung first marriages end in divorce. Subsequent alliances are forged by the couples' own desire to be married to one another, and are generally very stable

Relations between divorced individuals is usually quite amicable, with former partners living near one another and maintaining a cordial relationship.

Connection and conflict

The nature of marriage in !Kung society is uniquely adapted to this highly mobile society in which broad access to resources ensures ample food, and flexible band membership can provide "escape." Marriage is the major form of alliance formation between groups of !Kung, and friendly relationships with in-laws are crucial to survival. Given that mobility is a key feature in !Kung life, in-laws in other groups provide the assurance of another home when resources (and tempers) wear thin. A good marriage and good relations with in-laws is the best assurance of both individual and group survival. A n individual will never go hungry, and the group will never be riven by conflict from which one participant cannot literally simply walk away.

Lee (1984) has pointed out that without either material wealth or the aspiration for high status to generate conflict, it is usually marriage and sexual relations that provide the stage on which both conflict and alliance is played out. In fact, there has

been some speculation that the very young age at which girls were traditionally betrothed and married (sometimes as early as eight or nine) was in part to forestall conflicts arising in these two domains. Early marriage prevented rivalries among too many suitors. Moreover, if a girl were married before she became interested in courtship, it would be unlikely that she would have extramarital affairs. These conflicts are of no small significance: the most likely cause for a dispute which ends in murder, is arguing between men over their affections for the same woman.

Talking and telling tales

Marshall (1976:351), referring to the !Kung as "the most loquacious people," suggests that one useful strategy in maintaining peace and diffusing tensions is talking. People engage in conversation all day long, and well into the night. They talk as they work, as they eat, as they gather around the fires with their children at night, as they visit with other families. Often, people who have hunted or gathered separately during they day will recount in exhaustive detail the tracks of animals, amounts of berries, abundance of certain plants. They then plan the next days activities. Where might there be game? To whom will they give nuts?

Songs pepper the conversation, and can be used as a disciplinary measure, or to head off a conflict by warning an individual to correct inappropriate behavior. They compose songs specifically for this purpose, walk to the edge of the camp at night, and sing their disapproval.

In addition to the informal conversation that drives so much of !Kung daily life, there is a rich tradition of storytelling among the San. Most of these tales are set in a long-ago past, when people were not yet real humans, but animals, and many strange things that would never happen today were commonplace.

In some places, a few individuals are expert storytellers, known for their skills and set apart from others in this talent.

Among the !Kung, however, it is old people who are storytellers--and every old person rises to the occasion. Rather than gathering children around the fire to teach them the ways of the !Kung, elders are more content to spend time telling stories among themselves. Children listen informally; young adults do so with perhaps a little more intent. But storytelling is largely an activity "of a small group of old people getting together for some real grown-up enjoyment." (Biesele 1976:307) This is not because the older !Kung have no other way to fill what are increasingly emptier hours: storytelling is not "something *to* do when you are old" (because there are few other things to do) so much as "something *that* you do when you are old." (that is, a welcomed privilege bestowed by age.) (Biesele 1976:307)

Leadership and combat

It is clear that harmony is the linchpin to an adaptive !Kung life. The members of each band must cooperate and share within their corporate group. Marriage must establish strong and warm ties between families in different encampments, so that a pattern of reciprocal visiting is established, allowing movement between bands for personal or subsistence reasons.

The apparent harmony among the !Kung, not enforced by external authority, has been of great interest to outside observers. Richard Lee (1984) has endeavored to explain the ability of the !Kung to establish the order and peace that comes only "from the hearts and goodwill of the people themselves." (p. 87)

It seems logical to ask the question, Who is responsible for seeing that permission to hunt and gather in a territory is requested, and granted, and the balance of territorial use maintained, and disputes settled if access is denied?

Early accounts of the !Kung suggested that there was, in fact, the familiar role of "headman" or "big man" among the !Kung (Marshall 1969). This, in fact, is not the case. While individuals in each group do emerge in leadership positions, these are informal, and based not on an inherited right to such status, but rather owing to a modest demeanor, interpersonal skills, and successful handling of past conflicts.

While harmony is certainly the hallmark of traditional !Kung life, conflict--sometimes fatal --does occur. !Kung themselves describe three spheres of conflict: arguing, fighting, and deadly combat.

It is not surprising that among people who so enjoy talking and verbal jousting, arguments would ensue. Talking about food may lead to arguing about meat distribution. Talking about gifts may engender arguing about exchange. Often a conversation starts out as joking, only to escalate into something more serious as tempers flare. This culminates in a "talk," the rapid-fire hurling of insults, often sexual in nature, which may itself become a "fight."

Fighting involves two individuals, male or female, physically grappling with one another. They only last a few minutes before others pull them apart and hold them back until they calm down. Although wrestling and hitting may have occurred only moments before, after the two are separated they often joke with one another about their behavior. Matters are not always resolved so quickly, but there is ample opportunity for simply going away for a cooling off period

The potential for the most serious violence exists among men between the ages of twenty and fifty, who will resort to using poisoned arrows if pressed beyond their limits. The poison employed is very potent, and is fatal as often as not.

Hxaro exchange

The !Kung effectively employ talking and joking to avert the escalation of a fight, but perhaps the most important mechanism for maintaining goodwill is the hxaro exchange, a system of gift-giving which not only fosters friendly relations, but also serves to circulate goods and even maintain environmental balance.

The essence of hxaro is exchange between individuals that is not as immediate as barter: one person gives an item to another, and in the future an item is returned. The exact nature of the item--its equivalency in value--is of lesser importance than the consistency of give and take maintained in the relationship between the people involved. In attempting to learn the rules for hxaro, anthropologist Lee presented an informant with a string of questions as to the acceptability of items for exchange: in return for a spear, would five strings of beads be sufficient? Four? One? His !Kung informant laughed at Lee's desperation to understand the rules, saying, "I see what your problem is!...you don't understand our way. One string, five strings, any return would be all right. You see, we don't trade with things, we trade with people!" (1984:98)

All !Kung are eligible to enter into hxaro together, with the primary pathways emanating from a husband and wife, who exchange with their children, who exchange with their spouses, who then exchange with their own parents, thus solidifying bonds between families whose children have married. All manner of items are exchanged in hxaro, from glass beads and other craftwork to arrows, spear and knives, and even dogs. The only items restricted from hxaro exchange were food and people.

As visiting plays a central role in !Kung mobility and social ties, it is not surprising that hxaro exchange is a focal point in any visit. Not only does such gift-giving extend established relationships, it can also serve as a safety valve for diffusing conflict; going off to do hxaro can function as a valid excuse to leave a group when involved in escalating dissension. Further, hxaro ties established with other groups allow !Kung to effectively exploit the environment, by relocating when food sources become scarce in one area while remaining abundant in another.

RELIGION AND THE SUPERNATURAL

Gods

The !Kung have no single explanation for the origin of life on earth. They tell stories about a time at the beginning of the world when people and animals were the same, and all lived in one village under the guidance of an elephant, sometimes thought of as the "higher God." Many of their stories about their "lesser God" portrays him as a trickster, someone who is a practical joker of grand proportion, always leading people astray and causing trouble in the village.

Ghosts

The !Kung have successful strategies for coping with their environment and their relationships with one another. However, as in any human group, they have little or no control over natural forces. !Kung fall ill and die; adversity of all sorts is no stranger. They have devised ways to explain and understand these circumstances, and as is often the case, their explanations transcend the forces of nature.

It is the ancestral ghosts --the gangwasi--who are responsible for most of the illness and other misfortune that befalls their living kin. Gangwasi wait near the villages, and send their destruction. It may seem surprising that a people who, in life, live harmoniously together would attribute such evil intent to their loved ones once dead. The !Kung, explain this by saying that it is death that turns people bad. All people are good when alive. They believe, in fact, that the great affection that people feel for one another in life is what motivates their spirits to send illness and death to the loved ones they have left behind. For while the gangwasi have all they need--food, and clothing, and the company of other gangwasi--they do not have those they love the most. It is the intense longing to be reunited with their dearest kin whom they have left behind which compels the gangwasi to send illness and death.

Admittedly, not all gangwasi harbor the same degree of malevolence towards their living kin. Many !Kung live their lives relatively free from misfortune; others seem to meet sorrow and adversity at every turn. While this is difficult to explain, some !Kung postulate that it is misbehavior on the part of the living that engenders the ill-will of their own kin's gangwasi. One man suggested, "...we know [gangwasi] expect certain behavior of us. We must eat so, and act so. When you are quarrelsome and unpleasant to other people, and people are angry with you, the gangwasi see this and come to kill you. The gangwasi can judge who is right and who is wrong." (Lee 1984:107-8) Thus, avoidance of gangwasi's censure can also function as an effective measure of social control, acting to reinforce adherence to shared social norms.

The !Kung are far from helpless in defending themselves against the malevolent entreaties of the gangwasi. They possess a wide array of magical spells and healing herbs with which to counteract the gangwasi's attack. The most potent item in their armamentarium, however, is num, the healing energy that enables indigenous healers to enter a trance, and while in this state, effect a cure.

Healing

Lee (1984) asserts that the !Kung are not overly given to philosophizing about their gods and ghosts except at the prodding of an anthropologist. They are, however, quite concerned with the threat of illness and death, and have devoted much time and energy to addressing these challenges.

To become a healer is a grand aspiration of many, and the !Kung feel it is a status accessible to all. Nearly half the men and one-third of the woman are acknowledged as having the power to heal.

Although this power is not restricted, neither is it gained without great hardship and pain. Those who are too young, or too immature, are discouraged from attempting the long apprenticeship required to become a healer. The apprentice receives lessons from older, established healers who go into trance to teach the novices, rubbing their own sweat onto the pupil's healing centers--their bellies, backs, foreheads, and spines. The novices require frequent breaks, because it takes time for those less experienced to be able to manage the intense pain that is engendered by the healing power. They can only go so far; then they must rest, gather their resolve, and go on a little longer.

Healing is most often accomplished in the context of a !kia dance, beginning at sundown and continuing through the night. These are held several times a week, and are attended by all who are in the camp. While designed to effect healing, these dances accomplish other things. They provide a unifying experience for the whole community, as well as an outlet for grief and tension, hostility and fear. !Kia is the "primary expression of a religious existence and a cosmological perspective." (Katz 1976:286)

The !kia depends on the activation of num, which resides in the bellies of the women and men who are healers. When they dance, in preparation for entering a trance state to effect a cure, the substance heats up, and, boiling, travels up the healer's spine to explode with therapeutic power in the brain. One healer described it as "[boiling] in my belly and ... up to my head like beer. When the women sta[rt] singing and I start dancing, at first I f[eel] quite all right. Then, in the middle, [the] medicine begins to rise from my sto[mach]. After that I see all the people like [the] birds, the whole place will be s[pinning] around, and that is why we run[.] The trees will be circling also. [When] your blood become very hot, [the] blood boiling on fire, and then [comes] healing." (Lee 1984:109)

Women healers have [a] medicine, gwah, in their sto[mach and] kidneys. In the Drum Dance[,] tremble and they enter the !kia trance state. As they dance the gwah travels up the spine as num does, lodging in the neck. To gain the gwah power, women chop up the root of a short shrub, boil it into a tea, and drink it. They need not do this before every Drum Dance; the power they secure from the tea consumed at the beginning of their healing career is so strong that is lasts a lifetime.

Melvin Konner (1987), a medical anthropologist who investigated the healing practices of the !Kung before undertaking his own medical training in the United States, writes, in a compelling account of his time spent in both medical systems, of the great power in the !Kung men's healing ritual.

"Women sit in a circle around a small fire, clapping in complex rhythms and singing in a yodeling way. Men with rattles strapped to their legs dance around in a circle behind them, always in one direction, steadily, monotonously. Through a combination of dance, concentration, listening to the music, and practice, some of these men enter altered states of consciousness--trances--in which healing by the laying on of hands is believed to be possible.

In these trances the men take great risks and experience great pain--especially when they are learning. Their souls may leave their bodies never to return. Injury, pain, and death are part of the expected risk of learning to heal. Physically, when in trance, they may injure themselves by running at full tilt into the pitch-dark savannah, or by pouring glowing red coals over their heads. Furthermore, the medicine itself is said to boil up in the flanks of each healer, and this effect, essential for healing power, is said to cause a pain like no other. Spiritually, they believe that their souls leave their bodies when they are in this state. As mature healers they can use this phenomenon to advantage, arguing in the spirit-world on behalf of the ill person."

Konner (1987:373-4) writes of the !kia lessons that "the best insurance against the risks is the support of the community of healers. Trusting in your fellow-healers, especially your teachers, you can let go psychologically and spiritually; they will pull you away from the coals or prevent you from running into a tree; they will teach you how to turn the pain in your flanks into healing power; they will slowly bring your soul back into your body." This seems as though it could be said of the !Kung in more realms than healing. Lee (1984) has characterized them as a people with a sense of their own importance, a people of biting humor, and above all, the deepest regard for one another.

REFERENCES

BIESELE, M.
1976   Aspects of !Kung Folklore. in *Kalahari Hunter-Gatherers*. R.B. Lee and I. DeVore, eds. Cambridge:Harvard University Press.

KATZ, R.
1976   Education for Transcendence: !Kia-Healing with the Kalahari !Kung in *Kalahari Hunter-Gatherers*. R.B. Lee and I. DeVore, eds. Cambridge:Harvard University Press.

KONNER, M.
1987   *Becoming a Doctor*. New York: Viking.

LEE, R.B.
1979   *The !Kung San*. Cambridge: Cambridge University Press

LEE, R.B.
    1984   *The Dobe !Kung.* New
                York: Holt, Rinehart and
                Winston.

MARSHALL, L
    1976   Sharing, Talking and
                Giving: Relief of Social
                Tensions among
                the !Kung. in *Kalahari
                Hunter-Gatherers*. R.B.
                Lee and I. DeVore, eds.
                Cambridge:Harvard
                University Press.

§ THE BEGINNING

Long before the world began, there was Kiccemanito, the Great Spirit. He made wind and water, fire and rock; he made the sun and stars and Earth. To the Earth he gave tall trees and green plants. He created animals that ran on four legs, animals that flew, animals that swam, and last he created the people. Kiccemanito arranged all he created by the four sacred directions--north, south, west, and east-- and then two more: the sky above, and the earth below.

Not long after, the seas flooded the earth, and the animals tried to find it again, to no avail. One after the other, they searched beneath the seas, until finally the muskrat scraped a pawful of soil from the submerged earth, and from that scrap the world was recreated. Kiccemanito envisioned a purpose for the spirit of all he created. Trees would grow large and give shade and protection. Plants would flourish and give food and medicine. Animals would be bountiful and their lives offered up as

food and clothing for the people. But all this goodness would be recognized and appreciated by the people whose benefit it would serve. Nothing would be sacrificed without praise and thanks and a token of appreciation.

The people lived first by the great ocean in the east, but a vision carried them westward and following it, they found the Great Lakes.

This is the beginning of the Ojibwa's tale, the explanation of their creation and of finding their home.

OVERVIEW

The Ojibwa , a native American group living in the northern Midwest in the United States and south-central Canada, refer to themselves as Anishinabe, which literally means "human being," a term by which many of the world's people are known to themselves. There is some speculation and disagreement about the origin of the name Ojibwa. It has been said to refer to their style of moccasin ("ojibwa" meaning puckered up, and referring to the crimped stitching that edges the moccasins). Others (Tanner 1992) suggest that it is instead derived from "ojibiweg," which means "those who make pictographs," and that their name refers instead to the paintings on birch bark that were traditionally used as a form of writing.

Originally, an area extending north of Lakes Superior and Huron was home to the Ojibwa. Beginning in the seventeenth century, their geographical expansion resulted in a four-part division. These groups are the Salteaux (northern Ojibwa); the Plains Ojibwa, or Bungee; the Southeastern Ojibwa, and the Southwestern Chippewa. By the end of the eighteenth century the Salteaux occupied the Canadian Shield north of Lake Superior and south and west of Hudson and James Bays. This is a flat area of poor soil, and numerous lakes and swamps. Plains Ojibwa country, in Southern Saskatchewan and Manitoba, is a region forested with oak and ash, with great rolling hills. The Southeastern Ojibwa in Michigan's lower peninsula and adjacent areas of Ontario share an environment similar to that of the Southwestern Chippewa in northern Minnesota, extreme northern Wisconsin, and Ontario between Lake Superior and the Manitoba border. Both live in country of rolling hills, deciduous forests of maple, birch, poplar, and oak, marshes, prairie, rivers and lakes. They live with long, cold winters and short, hot summers.

The Ojibwa, one of the largest American Indian groups north of Mexico, numbered at least 35,000 in the mid-seventeenth century. Today the Ojibwa have been given one hundred or more small reservations in Michigan, Wisconsin, Minnesota, North Dakota, Montana and Oklahoma. The majority of the roughly 200,000 individuals live in the Canadian provinces of Ontario, Manitoba, and Saskatchewan.

HISTORY

In the mid-seventeenth century, the Ojibwa first encountered Europeans on their land. These explorers found an impressive natural bounty in rivers and forests. It wasn't long before the Gulf of St. Lawrence was crowded with fishing expeditions. The market for native furs-- mink, bear, wolf, otter, and beaver--was tremendous, and by the end of the century Ojibwa were heavily involved in the fur trade, and eager to expand their trade for European goods.

The burgeoning desire for European trade goods led to escalating inter-tribal conflict centering on the rights to exclusive fur-trading privileges, especially fierce between the Iroquois and the Huron. In the middle 1600s, the combined effect of Dutch-issued firearms and the decimation of newly-introduced diseases (smallpox chief among the epidemics) exacted a dramatic toll.

Earlier, the Ojibwa were closely allied to the Huron to their south. However, after the Huron were defeated by the Iroquois in their battle for control of the fur trade, the Ojibwa came under forceful Iroquois attack. In a successful attack that put an end to Iroquois power in their region, Ojibwa expanded both south and westward.

Eventually, representatives from fifteen Indian nations negotiated peace in the trade wars, but not without great cost. By the beginning of the eighteenth century Ojibwa culture had changed dramatically. Animals which had been hunted mainly for subsistence were now trapped primarily to be used in trade, and as dependence upon European trade good increased, traditional patterns and activities diminished.

Also with the development of the European fur trade, the exploitation of a particular hunting and trapping territory (which had been vaguely defined areas) evolved into discrete territories over which hunting and trapping groups had exclusive rights to fur resources. By the century's end their major geographical expansion resulted in the four part tribal fracturing.

With migration, too, came some significant modifications in traditional hunting, fishing, and gathering subsistence patterns. These modifications were most evident among the Northern Ojibwa, who adopted a subarctic cultural pattern, borrowing extensively from the Cree, and the Plains Ojibwa, who incorporated numerous aspects of Plains Indian culture.

During the first half of the nineteenth century, Ojibwa began to experience the influence of the American government. They became, once again, increasingly dependent on traders, this time Americans. While fishing was plentiful in the summertime, winter found the Ojibwa without large game, which had been depleted, and left them in need of provisions owned by traders. Large parcels of land were ceded in return for the promise of continued blacksmith service (upon which they had come to rely for gun and trap repair, as well as fishing spears and ice cutters); hunting and fishing rights on the land to be given up; and payments of salt and tobacco on an annual basis. Demands for farmland forced Southeastern Ojibwa to cede their territory, and the movement toward reservations began in earnest.

Canadian officials attempted what they termed a "civilization" program, aimed at redirecting Ojibwa life to a reservation-based farming economy, to replace traditional fishing, hunting and gathering. Missionaries across North America embraced the "civilization" programs as a way to facilitate conversion to Christianity, which appeared easier to effect with a population that was less dispersed. With harsh winters and a short growing season the copper-rich, forested land in Wisconsin and Minnesota was unsuitable for farming, and thus not in jeopardy of being ceded to agriculturalists by government decree. But Ojibwa resistance was challenged by copper miners and the lumbering industry, eager to exploit the abundant resources on Ojibwa land, and loath to allow the Ojibwa to remain living on land they had ceded, a right which had been granted them by the United States government.

In keeping with their plan for Ojibwa to adopt a farming economy, and under pressure from these burgeoning industries, the government attempted to resettle the Ojibwa west of the Mississippi where they could live in permanent shelters and farm the land. This initial attempt was unsuccessful, and an alternative program-- to allot individual parcels of land within reservations to individual families--was introduced. A series of treaty conferences ensued, during which Native American leaders presented their complaints: promised payments had not materialized; settlers on Ojibwa land had gone through the woods and taken the game that been left hanging on trees to cure; government financed schools were educating not Ojibwa children, but only those of the traders. Perhaps the point of most contention was presented by Ojibwa from Sault Ste. Marie, whose land was destroyed by the construction of a shipping canal. Unsuspecting villagers were taken by surprise as 400 workers arrived in their village, and began construction which destroyed not only fishing sites, but the village itself. Families were forced to flee their homes as the canal building proceeded.

Although treaties were signed promising permanent homes, farming acreage, equipment, and carpentry tools, this allotment process never came to fruition. By the time an official Act was passed into law, nearly 90% of the land promised to the Ojibwa and others was already owned and settled.

Despite their desire to maintain their way of life, Ojibwa resettled on reservations could neither fish nor gather wild rice on land unsuitable for these economies. Thus, consequences to Ojibwa culture, beginning with the earliest days of the fur trade, were cataclysmic. The technology introduced, the scattering and removal of the indigenous population, and the intertribal conflict engendered, had dramatic affects on Ojibwa culture.

Before the middle of the nineteenth century, Ojibwa tools were fashioned of stone and bone. Bowls and spoons, canoe paddles and sleds, drums and snowshoes were all made of wood. Birchbark provided the material for canoes and containers. Spears and bows and arrows were the tools of the hunt, with animal skins providing the material for clothing, blankets, and tailoring. Hooks and nets were used for fishing.

With the advent of the fur trade, iron tools (scissors, needles, axes, knives), cooking utensils (kettles and pots), as well as guns and alcohol, were introduced, with tremendous consequences. Iron tools transformed the approach to hunting. Pottery craft was reduced to obsolescence with the availability of sturdier and more efficient iron kettles. The European demand for fur coincident with governmental plans to encourage a shift from the traditional economy to one based on farming created an ironic dilemma: as Hallowell (1992:18) explains, "the continuing demand for furs, in the long run, entrenched most of these Indians more firmly in their occupation as hunters since so many of them were compelled to remain in a region where any transition to agriculture was impossible."

The European system of buying and selling introduced to the indigenous peoples a system of "debt" which was to them wholly unfamiliar. Goods were sold to hunters on credit, with payment in furs expected subsequently. European traders attempted to offset the risks inherent in giving goods on credit by establishing considerably higher prices for the goods they sold to the hunters. A host of factors, not the least of which was the unstable, seasonally changing availability of game, insured that native peoples were rarely able to escape perpetual indebtedness. While they were becoming more dependent upon trade goods, they were not able to incorporate the technology for producing or repairing such goods on their own, thus never able to benefit from the new technologies by employing them to become economically independent.

SETTLEMENTS

Ojibwa patterns of movement and settlement were guided largely by the seasons, and varied among groups as their environments varied. In general, bands dispersed in the winter, moving to hunting grounds where deer, moose, bear, and a variety of small game were available. In the spring, maple trees were tapped, and the sap was gathered and boiled to produce maple syrup. Early Ojibwa established semipermanent villages in the summer and maintained temporary camps during the rest of the year, in keeping with their need to move in order to efficiently exploit fish, game, and wild plant resources.

While the strategy of seasonal settlement and movement was found to some degree in all the Ojibwa groups, it was differently elaborated in each. Southeastern Ojibwa and Southwestern Chippewa returned to permanently established summer village bases to plant gardens. Plains Ojibwa were highly mobile, and moved to the open plains in the summertime to hunt the bison herds upon which they focused their economy and whose skins were used to construct their familiar tipis.

The Northern Ojibwa spent the late fall, winter, and spring moving in dispersed winter hunting groups. As the ice melted, these small groups met up with other such bands, spending the summer months congregated in fishing settlements. In contrast to the isolation of winter hunting movement, the assembly of large groups at fishing sites afforded the opportunity to renew social ties and perform important communal ceremonies. In addition, many of these summer sites were near trading posts, where supplies could be secured for the coming year.

During the summer months spent in the villages, the gathering of wild nuts and berries, and planting of small gardens of maize, beans, squash, and pumpkins supplemented fishing. Wild rice, available most easily to the Southeastern Ojibwa, was harvested in the fall.

KINSHIP AND SOCIOPOLITICAL ORGANIZATION

Despite the fact that there was seasonal movement, sometimes of small groups, these smaller units of Ojibwa belonged to a larger whole. In earliest times, the Ojibwa were organized into small autonomous bands of interrelated families. As is characteristic of band organization , these were flexible groups with an egalitarian structure. Band size and characteristics varied somewhat among different groups. Southeastern Ojibwa and Southwestern Chippewa bands were made up of several hundred people; northern Ojibwa bands were smaller, each numbering about 50-75 individuals. Plains Ojibwa bands tended to be looser, more shifting units.

Kinship terms, used as both reference and address, functioned not only to identify the relationship of one person to another. They were also a vehicle to guide behavior, and express the content of role relations and expectations. (For example, a child came to recognize that those men addressed by his father as "brother" all act towards the child as his own father might.) Beginning with earliest childhood, kinship terms directed social interaction, allowing relations with both extended family and members of other groups as they moved among them.

Generally, Ojibwa society was organized into a number of exogamous totemic clans, with membership reckoned patrilineally. (Northern Ojibwa in the Berens River area of Manitoba were more likely to be endogamous.) Because these clans were not localized, most individuals could depend on finding some members of their own clan in any settlement to which their summer movement took them. Marriages , which involved little formal ceremony, were generally arranged by parents or guardians. Cross-cousin marriage, while practiced, was not preferred; most marriages were monogamous, although polygyny was possible.

Ojibwa political organization was, like other aspects of their sociocultural system, dramatically influenced by contact with European fur traders.

Traditionally, there were no powerful political "chiefs" among the Ojibwa. However, European traders sought to identify an individual within each band with whom they could negotiate. One

individual was designated by a trader, and an official relationship was structured between the two men, a vitally important link for the trader whose livelihood depended on maintaining this access to pelts. As a result of the status granted and attention paid to the "chief," this individual gained status and prestige, which were reinforced by goods he was given to distribute as gifts. This newly defined position, "a convenient means of dealing with Indians whose native culture did not function through persons whose role it was to represent them in transactions with outsiders," was instituted among all of the Ojibwan groups. (Hallowell 1991:35)

Among the eighteenth century Southeastern Ojibwa, bands were headed by less formal chiefs; as farming and more permanent settlement patterns were encouraged by the government, an elected chief, assistant chiefs, and a local council became the characteristic local political organization. Among the Northern Ojibwa, the individual selected for band leadership was usually a skilled trader whose kin group formed the basis of the band's membership. Plains Ojibwa bands had several chiefs, with one recognized as the head chief and secondary chiefs designated based on hunting skills, achievements in battle, generosity, and leadership ability. Elected councilors assisted the chiefs.

As Hallowell points out, the power held by these chief and councilors was derived primarily from their function as trade representatives, but this authority did not extend to matters arising within their "bands," which were also groups that were conceived largely by government agencies. Groups that were defined by the people themselves did not correspond to those conceptualized by traders and government officials. To the Ojibwa, the true seat of individual power was to be found in the indigenous healers, whose abilities acquired through dreams were truly matters of life and death.

OJIBWA CULTURE

The belief system of the Ojibwa turns on the important relationship between people and those who are other-than-people. While skills and knowledge obtained from fellow Ojibwa are certainly important, there are crucial aspects of a successful life which can only be known and achieved through dependence upon those who are not human. Hallowell reports that he found "neither myth, tale, nor tradition [portraying] a human being as making any discovery, bringing about any change, or achieving any status or influence unaided by other than human persons." (1991:80)

To understand this one must first understand that in the Ojibwa conceptualization there is no sharp division between the natural and the supernatural, as defined by the Western scientific cultural model. There are animate and inanimate objects. The latter category is made up largely of manufactured items (although pipes are spoken of as animate); plants, fish, animals and humans beings are all classified as animate, as are the sun and wind and other elements. Also found among the category of animate beings are those animals which are known to exist but are rarely, if ever, seen. These include Large Snakes, Great Frogs, and Big Turtles. Of even greater importance are the Thunder Birds, whose wings make the sound of the thunder, and whose blinking eyes are the accompanying lightning. Thunder Birds are classified with other birds whose migratory patterns correspond to the stormy seasons during which thunder and lightning occur.

All plants and animals are controlled by their "owners," whose permission was an absolute prerequisite to securing them through hunting or gathering. This belief meant that skillful techniques and an exhaustive knowledge of their environment were necessary but not sufficient talents for successful subsistence. To know the owners of each species, and to make certain that each plant and animal was correctly treated was the only insurance against failure. The remains of an animal, who would be killed only for a useful purpose, must be disposed of and honored with proper ceremonial respect. Failure to accord plants and animals this right would inevitably result in retribution by the owner, generally the inability to secure that plant or animal again in the future. A hunter had a relationship with the owner of the species he hunted; the "use" of an animal resulted in a debt owed the species' owner, and such obligations must be fulfilled. Likewise, when plants were gathered, owners must be properly addressed and an offering (usually of tobacco) was left in the ground.

To the Ojibwa, the category of "persons" includes not only themselves-- anishinabe: human beings--but also "people"--that is, animate beings-- who are decidedly persons, although not human. These beings are more powerful than human beings, and might be classified as "supernatural" beings in another cultural context. These persons are referred to as "our grandfathers" by the Ojibwa, who from childhood have knowledge and experience with these beings. They have a real place in the lives of Ojibwa, through myth, and ceremony, and dreams.

Myths told about "our grandfathers" were thought to be heard not only by the people assembled to listen, but by the objects of the stories themselves. It is believed that their delight in hearing them was so great that long ago, one urged the others: "We'll try to make everything suit the Indians so long as any of them exist, so that they will never forget us and always talk about us." (Hallowell 1991:66)

Tales told about the "grandfathers" were generally told by elders--human grandparents--who were revered members of society. They educated adults and children alike, teaching, through myths and dance and song those parts of wisdom deemed every bit as important as the practical skills of hunting, sewing, cooking and fishing. Children, raised with little strictness and rarely reprimanded or punished, were in the care of women and elders for the first years of their lives. Boys of seven began to be instructed by adult men in the ways of hunting and fishing; girls continued to be instructed about domestic life by their mothers. When an Ojibwa girl received the "gift... denied to men" (Tanner 1992:27)--her first menstruation--she became a woman, leaving the village for a time, and returning with a new status. Special instruction was afforded to those young women and men who displayed the gift of healing powers, the gift to be among the Midé.

Religion and View of the World:

Ojibwa religion is bound up with several distinctive features: dreaming, fasting, visions, and, above all else, the relationship with "the grandfathers," the other-than-human beings.

According to Hallowell, "faith in the power of the other than human persons, trust in the essential help they can offer human beings, and dependence upon them in order to achieve a good life define the ...core of Ojibwa religion." (1991:81). Religious beliefs that emphasize this critical relationship direct behavior, and thus function as a primary way of maintaining the social order.

The primary contact between individuals and these other beings is achieved during dreaming, a state of primary importance in Ojibwa life. It is during dreams that power is given and received, and while contact can be made with "the grandfathers" outside of dreams, it is only in the dreaming state that the most intimate and powerful relationship is forged.

Just as a sharp dichotomy between the natural and the supernatural can not be effectively drawn for the Ojibwa, neither can experience gained through waking and dreaming teachings be set in opposition. The world experienced while dreaming is not one of fantasy and unreality; it is another occasion for reflective thought. One difference between the experiences of sleep and waking, however, is the ability of the soul during sleep to break free of the body, allowing the most intense contact with other than human beings. During such contact, "blessings" of knowledge, and, thus, power, are bestowed; and beginning in early childhood, one was encouraged to dream in order to receive these blessings.

To facilitate visionary dreams, boys especially were encouraged in a fast, during which time they would be visited by "the grandfathers." During this state, the fasting boy would be approached by one who would take him under his wing and tutelage, whom he could see and hear. The fasting period might last a week before such "guardian spirits" would appear; the boy's father or grandfather might appeal to their own long-ago recognized teachers to help secure the boy's own blessing.

Once secured, the vision was not discussed. In fact, if a boy began to discuss his experience, or ask for guidance in interpreting what he had dreamt, he was cautioned against it; seeking clarification through discussion of one's vision might be grounds to lose the blessing and the power it bestowed. A dreamer's family was made aware obliquely of the fast's fruition by a boy's change in behavior. He became somewhat withdrawn and introspective, observed new ritual obligations assumed to have been demanded of him in his dream. His proud family let his achievement be known to the rest of the community, but also only inferentially: they had found him in an altered state of consciousness, his manner had changed, they had seen differences in his behavior.

Dreams and visions varied greatly, in both content and intensity, from person to person. Some "dream visitors" impart only knowledge and access to trapping and fishing. Others to warfare. Still others imparted the skills necessary for curing. One person may be visited by many guardian spirits; others may never fulfill their quest for a vision. Whether blessed by many or none, the dreamer was to remain equally silent, both because boasting is unacceptable and because it jeopardizes ones ability to hold on to the power received.

It has been suggested that one reason that Ojibwa feel a strong link between humans and the other-than-human spirits that are "the grandfathers," is that both classes of persons are bound by the same moral order. Primary among these shared values is the importance of mutual exchange. The guardian spirits give blessings and knowledge to their human grandchildren: they have an excess of power, more than they need, and thus they must share it.

The egalitarian focus that serves to distribute goods and services in a society without a market economy also guides the act of sharing across human and non-human boundaries. The accumulation of excess goods, indicative of greed, is as unbefitting to "the grandfathers" as it is to those who dream of them. Self-deprivation can be taken to excess as much as over-acquisitiveness. One boy was reported to have been dissatisfied with the blessing he received during his initial fasting vision. His desire was to know everything in the world, to dream of every leaf on every tree so he could see beyond them to know all. He continued to fast. This desire, considered greedy, was granted, but with the proviso that as the leaves fell from the tree, so too would the boy fall ill. And when the trees were at last bare, his life too would end. As Hallowell explains, "Overfasting is considered as greedy as hoarding. It violates a basic moral value of the cosmic society of the Ojibwa." (1991:92)

In keeping with the rights and duties bound up in sharing and reciprocity, the blessings received during the dreams were not bestowed without obligation. If one was to utilize the knowledge and power obtained through vision to their fullest extent, both prohibitions and "debts" must be attended to. In some cases, food taboos were imposed by guardian spirits who were owners of that animal species. In others, items of clothing or adornment associated through myth with the bestower of ones blessings must be worn. Often contact was forbidden between the dreamer and certain other individuals. None of these observances may be explained; consequently, recipients of blessings often are forced to endure misunderstanding by others, requiring the

exercise of great self-control. Infractions result not only in the withdrawal of the blessing; even unintentional violation of such taboos extracted a penalty, usually illness. Any breach of conduct between people or between humans and other-than-humans is punished eventually: there is no comfort to be taken in the passage of time. "Bad conduct...'will keep following you.' Sooner or later you will suffer because of it." (Hallowell 1991: 93) Moreover, it may be those closest to you who will pay the price for your own infraction; it may be your children who fall ill and die.

Thus, the fear of falling ill functions, in traditional Ojibwa society, as a powerful sanction against behavior that fails to conform to that which is expected. Ethnographers have pointed out that this set of beliefs --grounded in individual responsibility for behavior, and a commitment to exercise self-control without explanation--acted against the acceptance of the government-introduced system of chiefdoms, which sought to impose sanctions by dictum from without.

In those settings where illness functions as a check on anti-social behavior, becoming ill has ramifications on two levels: not only as personal misfortune, but as a clear indicator of some moral or behavioral transgression against wider cultural values. This is further reinforced by the public disclosure of the violation that has brought on the illness. A confession of sorts is a necessary element in the curative process: once the misconduct has been identified and made known, it functions as a warning to others.

In their elegant recounting of Ojibwa myths, Overholt and Callicott (1982) alert the reader of these tales to some of the important elements out of which they are spun. It is through the telling of the myths that central values are passed on from Ojibwa to Ojibwa; for people outside of their tradition, examining the themes contained within the stories can be a window into the Ojibwa world.

Power is a recurrent theme in Ojibwa life; especially the power possessed and granted by the "grandfathers." One power possessed by persons and other-than-persons alike is that of metamorphosis, the changing of ones shape. Hallowell counts this as "one of the distinctive generic attributes of persons in Ojibwa thought." (1991:.66-7) This thought is never more in evidence than when considering the bestowal of blessing, through dreams and visions. These are parts of life and awareness that are no less real than the more mundane pieces of ones day; and surely no less powerful. The Ojibwa view of themselves as not solely people who live with other people, but as human beings who live in a more broadly defined society, with other-than-human persons, is exemplified in two other features of Ojibwa culture: the Midéwiwin, or Grand Medicine Society, and the shaking tent.

The Shaking Tent

The shaking tent (or shaking lodge) is a performance aimed at divining information not available through other means. Most often the questions asked have to do with the diagnosis and treatment of illness, the welfare of loved ones far away, or the location of game animals. The practice involves persons and powers from all the important realms of the Ojibwa world: the audience of Ojibwa, the "spirits" to be contacted, and the diviner.

In preparation for the event, a structure is erected. Poles are lashed together to form a barrel-shaped tent, or lodge, with skins, canvas, or birchbark draped over the framework. The diviner enters the tent after dark with the assembled audience outside. Songs and drumming are the vehicles by which the diviner calls his spirits to him. These are never a random assemblage of visitors whom he importunes: they are his own pawaganak, his own guardians.

The evidence of their arrival is the movement of the tent, which shakes from side to side with their appearance within. At times this movement is rendered even more impressive by the binding, hand and foot, of the diviner. Thus tied with rope, it could not be he creating the rhythmic motion. Hallowell (1991) tells of a diviner of such potency that he was said to have

requested that four tents be constructed. He placed articles of his clothing in three, and himself entered the fourth. Once he had begun his songs, all four tents began to sway.

It is not only the movement of the tent that signals the arrival of the pawaganak; they can also be heard to respond to the diviner's song with singing of their own. In addition to guardian spirits, the souls of those living persons being inquired about can visit the tent to offer information and advice. These voices and songs are not believed to be "channeled" through the diviner; they speak for themselves. While it is true that sometimes their voices could be heard by the audience outside the tent and sometimes not, they are always intelligible to the diviner who, though he may be interpreting them, is surely not creating them. (Brown and Brightman 1988:153)

The Midéwiwin

One of the best known features of rich Ojibwa culture is the Midéwiwin (literally "mystic doings") of the Midé (mystic) Society, sometimes referred to as the Grand Medicine Society.

The Midéwiwin is an organized society of men and women who possess the knowledge to cure by the use of plants and herbs. Initiates, who have experienced a vision in which curing powers have been imparted, must serve an extended apprenticeship, during which they are tutored, for a price, by an established Midé priest.

Much of the accumulated knowledge of the Midéwiwin--stories, songs, and dances--were inscribed as pictographs on birchbark scrolls. After sufficient time, the aspiring Midé member participates in an initiation ceremony, during which he or she is "shot" with a white shell, ordinarily carried in the medicine bag of a member. Participants, in trance and falling unconscious after this magical shot, regained consciousness to spit the powerful shell from their mouths.

The earliest accounts of the Midéwiwin portray it as far more than a vehicle for curing illness. Beliefs about illness and curing in general reflect, as do other aspects of Ojibwa belief and practice, an individualism found at the core of Ojibwa culture. Ojibwa religion has been called "very much an individual affair," focused as it was on the personal experience through visions and dreams of an individual, which resulted in a unique relationship forged between one person and a guardian spirit (or, in some cases, spirits). So too, illness is believed to be caused by sorcery or as retribution for misconduct toward the "grandfathers" or ones fellow humans. While certainly important in the realm of solidarity among Ojibwa, it also has a strong flavor of singularity.

There are several categories of shamans, or professional healers, among the Ojibwa, quite apart from the Midé priests of the Midéwiwin. These other healers received their gifts as individual blessings, bestowed upon them during dreaming or visions. Once learned, this medical knowledge is "private property, the visionary or dream inspiration of specific medicines and techniques [exhibiting] a high degree of individualism and variation." (Brown and Brightman 1988:174)

This individualism did not exclude the practitioners in the Midéwiwin: there was no standard curriculum taught to all their members either, no remedy known to all, leading to the interchangeability of practitioners so common to Western biomedicine. When asked about a cure, a Midé priest might reply, "I can tell you about my own medicines. I do not know about other people's medicines..." (Brown and Brightman 1988:174)

Thus, those early writers (for example, Schoolcraft 1851) describing the Midéwiwin characterize it as transcending the limits of its curing responsibilities, having national participation and engendering national pride. Others who observed the rites emphasized what they regarded as its unifying aspects: "Every person who had been initiated into the secrets of this mysterious society ...[was] imperatively obliged to be present on every occasion when its grand ceremonies were solemnized. This created yearly a national gathering, and ... bonds which united one member to another." (Hickerson 1988:56)

In recent years, there has been reexamination of the Midéwiwin and its origin and place in Ojibwa history. It had earlier been assumed to represent an aboriginal institution--that is, to have been part of Ojibwa culture arising from within its own tradition, present before contact with outside groups. This assumption has been challenged by more recent anthropological investigation.

Ojibwa culture and society, along with that of other native peoples, was forced to undergo major changes during European contact. One consequence of stressful contact, which challenges traditional patterns of both belief and behavior, is the appearance of "nativistic" or "revitalization" movements. The most well-known of these include Melanesian cargo cults, the Ghost Dance of western native peoples, and the Handsome Lake religion of the Iroquois.

It is the contention of anthropologist Harold Hickerson (1988) that the Midéwiwin, rather than originating in pre-contact times, is in fact another example of such a phenomenon. In a thoughtful and well-supported treatise, he details the evidence for his claim that the Midéwiwin among the Ojibwa and other groups emerged out of a reaction to the challenges of Christianity and European contact, and that its ceremonies "represented and reflected new modes of organization, not ancient ones." (p. 63)

OJIBWA TODAY

Historical descriptions of the Ojibwa detail the traditional life of the past. But in many ways, the current experience of modern Ojibwa are portrayed in them too. The rich cultural heritage of the people who call themselves anishinabe survives through their continuing celebration of themselves in art, language, and ceremony.

OJIBWA

Following the Great Depression in the United States, the economy of the Ojibwa suffered along with that of the rest of the nation, only to rebound during World War II. Ojibwa joined other native peoples in moving to urban areas and laboring variously in shipyards, factories, and aircraft plants for the war effort. As Tanner (1992) points out, however, diversion of funds to the military from domestic programs had an adverse effect on schools, roads, and hospitals on the reservation.

In the 1950s, a government relocation program attempted to reduce reservation living (thus government expenses) by urging native Americans to migrate to urban areas and assimilate into mainstream American society. Nearly half of the native population of Minnesota had been relocated to urban areas by the middle of the 1970s.

It was also during the 1970s, however, that government policy began to become more sensitive to the needs and desires of Native Americans, and both laws and funds began to be aimed at preserving traditional culture. Alternative schools offering instruction in Ojibwa language and beginning the day with traditional ceremonial observances came into existence. Ojibwa tribal councils provided scholarship money for students to attend universities, where they increasingly found programs allowing them to continue learning about their own heritage and culture.

While the Ojibwa people are not a homogeneous group, there is still widespread adherence to traditional values and culture. Oral literature, art and craftwork, language and religion are still passed along to new generations. Hunting, gathering, and fishing continues. Tanner reminds us, that "in ceremonies, dancing, and drumming, they are still Anishinabe." (1992:111).

REFERENCES

BROWN, J.S.H. AND R. BRIGHTMAN

1988   *The Orders of the Dreamed.* St Paul: Minnesota Historical Society Press.

HALLOWELL, A.I. AND J.S.H.BROWN
1992   *The Ojibwa of Berens River, Manitoba.* Fort Worth: Harcourt Brace Jovanovich

HICKERSON, H.
1988   *The Chippewa and their Neighbors.* Prospect Heights: Waveland Press.

OVERHOLT, T.W. AND J.B.CALLICOTT
1982   *Clothed-In-Fur and Other Tales.* Lanham: University Press of America.

TANNER, H.H.
1992   *The Ojibwa.* New York: Chelsea House.

§ THE BEGINNING

In the beginning the earth was flat, and dark, and silent. No hills or valleys, no trees or rivers. No birds called; no sun shone.

Out of the ground rose an old, old woman. She was blind, and in her arms she carried three babies: two girls and one boy. Across the land she crawled, clutching her children, and in the furrows left by her knees fresh water bubbled up. She turned westward and formed the shores. She crawled further and created the ports.

After a time she thought perhaps she was making the island too large; so she journeyed northward to create the straights that separate the islands where we are. On her last journey, she did the final thing: she separated the land of the Tiwi from all others. Before she crawled away--we do not know where--she turned back to create green on the bare land, and animals. Because here she was leaving her children; and her children must have food.

INTRODUCTION AND HISTORY

The Tiwi occupy Melville and Bathurst Islands, which form a cultural as well as geographical unit. Taken together, they span about three thousand square miles. Located off the north coast of Australia, they lie about thirty miles north of Darwin.

The land is generally flat, with a low central ridge on Melville Island rising to about three hundred feet, and running west to east. Along this ridge running south to north are nine rivers which flow north to the sea. Along the headwaters of the larger rivers are open marshlands; on the northern and especially the southern coasts are areas of sandy beach and rocky cliffs.

On Bathurst, which boasts less elevation, rivers are small and largely tidal. Both islands are heavily forested, characterized largely by mangrove forests, mixed eucalyptus and cypress, woolly-butt, ironwood, and string-bark. As is found on the mainland, marsupials --wallaby, opossum, bandicoot--are present in large numbers. Snakes and lizards abound, and fruit bats populate the mangrove swamps. Crocodiles pose great danger both in rivers and on the coast. Monsoons occur between November and March, while little or no rain falls from June to September.

Northern people most likely came into contact with outsiders before those living to the south. It has been suggested, for example, that the coastal region of Arnhem Land probably hosted Indonesian fishing expeditions hundreds of years before British contact. Aided by north-west monsoon winds, these fishing parties most likely depended upon native Australian labor in their exploitation of the rich beche-de-mer fishing grounds. These individuals did not settle in the islands: when after several months the monsoonal winds blew homeward, they returned. In Queensland, native populations probably had contact with the peoples of New Guinea.

The Tiwi, too, most probably had contact with outsiders long ago, although definitive records are not available. Perhaps sailors blown off course landed accidentally (Goodale 1971). The Dutch, during the seventeenth century, sighted and named the islands which are home to the Tiwi. In the eighteenth century the Portuguese seized native Australians from the northern coast as slaves. The nineteenth century brought Malay fishing parties and Japanese pearlshell collectors.

It was during the early part of the nineteenth century that French exploration and British occupation brought intensive Western contact. The first foreign settlement was a British establishment (Fort Dundas) which was abandoned after five years of hardship. It was not for another seventy five years that further European settlement was attempted. In the early twentieth century, Catholic missions were established on the southeastern coast of Bathurst Island, and in the years following there was growing contact with white Australians.

In 1986 the Tiwi population totaled roughly two thousand, with Bathurst Island home to about 1300; and two Melville island townships totaling 700.

SUBSISTENCE

Native Australians were traditionally hunters and gatherers. While there are overall similarities among native groups--to a much larger extent, for example, than among the very different tribal people of Africa--there are also differences.

The Tiwi live in a varied environment which provides them with dietary abundance today as it did in the past. This generous supply of fish, game and vegetable foods is connected very firmly to what may be the most familiar characteristic of Tiwi culture: their system of marriage. Nanda (1991) points out that polygyny, among the Tiwi, appears to be adaptive to these foragers much in the same way it is in horticultural societies.

Men hunt turtles, geese, lizards, fish, and wallabies, all of which are in ready supply. However, as is typical of foraging subsistence, it is the edible plants, fruits, and vegetables gathered by women which make up the bulk of the daily food supply. In addition to providing the gathered items which are the staple of daily meals, women also hunt small game, using tools that they manufacture. There is no problem securing food in the Tiwi environment; however, the collection of the abundantly available supplies does pose a challenge, as it demands many hands

The traditional day began with women and children fanning out to begin the day's subsistence activities. Typically, only younger men hunted and fished. Young boys and older men participated least in daily foraging activities.

Increasingly after European settlement, Tiwi became employed in a variety of jobs related to settlement life, including education, health, community service, and government. While each community has a shop where food and other material goods may be purchased, the majority of Tiwi are concerned with the maintenance of hunting and foraging skills among the young. With a preference for "bush" food over "store-bought" goods, Tiwi still make up much of their weekly diet with native foods.

Settlement

Modern-day Tiwi live in two to four bedroom houses built by outside contractors during the past fifteen to twenty years, complete with kitchen and bathrooms, electricity, and plumbing. Some families, settling on the land owned by their own local group, have built housing for themselves.

Traditionally, however, Tiwi set up camp in a cleared area around a fire, with the kind of shelter constructed dependent largely on the season. During the rainy season, which lasted from early November through late April, sheets of bark were stripped from trees and supported on wooden poles. During the dry season, shelters were needed only to provide shade, and were constructed by merely leaning leafy branches together.

Every Tiwi woman and man owns land, and thus has a landowning name. While the boundaries (and number) of these "countries" have changed many times over the past hundred years since their demarcation was first recorded, whichever group claims hold over an area has distinct responsibilities. In 1976, the islands were deeded back to the Tiwi under the Land Rights Bill, which created a Tiwi Land Council. The council recognizes seven countries, each represented by delegates. One is considered to own the land owned by one's father (although in the past, ownership of the land was conferred by one's father's burial in the land). All the individuals recognized as owners of a country are collectively held responsible for its maintenance: this includes not only natural but also spiritual resources. It is further expected that both knowledge of the land, and responsibility for that country, will be passed on to the next generation.

SOCIAL ORGANIZATION

The word "tiwi," in their own distinctive tongue, distantly related to other native Australian languages, means "people." As is the case with many indigenous names, it refers not to the human species but rather means "real" people, or primary beings. Traditionally, Tiwi referred to themselves by names indicating their membership in one of several landowning groups (which they call countries).

A key feature in the history of the Tiwi was their isolation. Reports of first contact between Tiwi and all other outsiders are characteristically quite hostile, and even fatal to the unfortunate visitors. Hart, et al (1988:10) point out that this feeling of being "distinct from any other alleged human beings who might show up from time to time on the beaches" and the accompanying feeling that these others were, in fact, "[excluded] from real 'human-ness'" (ibid) may account for their bellicose reception.

Because they were so isolated and rarely disturbed, Tiwi thought less of protecting or identifying their group as a whole; the unit within which they functioned on a daily basis was the band. Bands were large (typically one hundred individuals) and tended to move in a dispersed fashion, so that fellow members might not see one another for weeks. As is typically the case, Tiwi bands were characterized by flexible and often-shifting membership.

Hunting and gathering activities were organized as a band; but the focus of the daily routine was the household, which were fairly autonomous units of production and consumption. Often it was one household which decided where to set up camp, and when to break camp and move on. This autonomy was especially likely in larger domestic units, such as those belonging to a big man. Hart et al (1988:37) write of one such household as constituting "a complete community in itself, with the old man as executive director. He laid down the daily, weekly, and monthly work and travel schedules for the women, the young men, and the children. Most of the time the work went automatically because all the adults and the older children knew their jobs."

A distinction is drawn between a residential group--that is, the people who live in a particular locale together for a time--and a landholding group--meaning those to whom a "country" belongs. Residential members of a group have rights of access to the resources around them, come to the aid of members of other households in their residential group (for example, during times of conflict), and carry out certain ceremonial responsibilities (as, for example, when there is a death in the group). Rights of landholding, acquired through ones father, may extend beyond the residential unit, if ones father lived or died and was buried in a "country" of which he was not also an owner.

Kinship

Tiwi belong to their mother's matrilineal descent group, which they call their "skin." This matrilineal clan is a group whose members reckon their common descent from a group of unborn spirit beings living in or near a body of water. The traditional belief system explains pregnancy as occurring when a man discovers one of these unborn spirits and sends it to his wife, whose clan origin must be the same as the spirit's. Members of each of these named clans, further grouped into 4 larger exogamous units, provide one another with both moral and practical support. For every individual, it is important to recognize two clans: one' own clan (that of one's mother), and ones father's clan, from whom one chooses an individual to marry.

In the social system of the Tiwi, everyone is, at base, kin to everyone else. Kinship terms can be extended to every member of the population. The most basic division of kin is between those who are "close" (geographically) and those who are "far away" (called long-way kin).

Marriage

Customs surrounding Tiwi marriage have undergone enormous change in modern times, largely due to the influence of Catholic missionaries settling on the islands after World War II. However,

traditional marital patterns are of crucial importance in understanding the larger Tiwi social, political, and economic system.

Traditional Tiwi culture mandated that all women must be married. This belief is a more extreme version of the belief held by Australian mainland tribes, in which marriage is expected, but not required--and certainly not contracted for before birth. Thus, in the past, every female was at all times married. From birth--in fact, before birth--to death, there was no concept of an unmarried female. (In fact, there was no word in Tiwi language to convey this state, even about a newborn girl.)

To begin to understand this mandate, one must first understand the indigenous beliefs about conception. Again, the Tiwi shared with mainlanders the belief that a woman becomes pregnant because a spirit enters her body. A man has no physical role in the creation of a child. But the Tiwi took another step, in order to handle the potentially dangerous lack of predictability demonstrated by these impregnating spirits. Because a spirit could impregnate any female at any time, if every female were always married, every child could be assured a father. Thus, as soon as a baby girl was born, she was betrothed. (If she had not been already: in most cases, when girls reached puberty their "future" daughters were betrothed.) Women who were widowed did not leave the graveside of their husband without a new spouse.

The consequences of such a system are many; not the least of which is that at any given time, the entire female population--but only part of the male population--was married. As is found in most human groups, there is a roughly equal number of males and females born to the Tiwi. Consequently, this situation mandates a high degree of plural marriage.

It falls to a baby girl's father to betroth his infant daughter, and he does this with an eye to his own future economic, political, and social advantage. Baby girls are not promised to baby boys: Hart et al (1988:19) comment, "Put bluntly, in Tiwi culture daughters were an asset to their father, and he invested these assets in his own welfare." Therefore, he chose either someone who was an important friend or ally, or whom he wished to engage as a friend or ally. This might very likely be a man of his own age, perhaps one who had already promised a daughter to him. If this were the case, such an individual would be at least thirty or forty years older than his bride. A father also used this process to grant him security on his old age: rather than a man as old as himself, he might choose a man in his twenties who showed great promise of one day becoming an influential and wealthy man. The father could then be assured that by the time his daughter was old enough to comply with the bargain, he would have a wealthy son-in-law obligated to care for him in his waning years.

The intricacies of daughter bestowal go far beyond this description. Suffice it to say that ordinarily, a Tiwi girl was old enough to take up residence and act as a wife at about age fourteen. Her husband would generally be about forty. The arrival in his household of his first resident wife was usually followed quickly by two or three others. This is because after one father of a newborn girl had surveyed the prospects and set his stock in one young man, other fathers were likely to decide to do the same, based on their trust in the original bestower's "research." This was the first step to any man becoming a "big man:" once his wives were in residence he was assured future babies that he could bestow upon others.

A man's list of wives was, of course, always longer than the actual wives in residence. He continued to receive bestowals of baby girls well into his seventies, and it was not unusual for a man to die while the last of his promised wives were still infants. What becomes of the wives he has left behind, both those he has been living with, and those too young to have yet joined him? No female must ever be without a husband. And what of men upon whom babies are not bestowed? It is widow remarriage which solved both of these problems.

Bestowal was the primary method of acquiring young wives. But since widows had to be immediately remarried, those Tiwi men who were nor regarded as the most promising hunters or most likely to succeed in acquiring big man status could depend on marrying widows, who in some cases would still be quite a bit younger than themselves.

Catholic missionaries were successful in putting an end to the majority of polygynous marriages, unions between people of vastly different ages, and all childhood (and pre-natal) betrothals. By the middle 1950s, a young woman (sometimes with the guidance of her father) would identify an individual whom she would like to marry, and negotiations would begin. Widows are no longer encouraged to remarry: in fact, widows whose fathers are alive are encouraged not to remarry, but to join their father's households instead, and help care for them.

Tiwi wives

Bestowal of infant daughters and immediate remarriage of all widows resulted in households in which successful old men had as many as twenty wives, while men younger than thirty had none. Men who were between thirty and forty had wives who were elderly widows. This is an unusual household structure, but one which linked together all the aspects of Tiwi culture--kinship, subsistence, politics, economics, and law.

The Tiwi explicitly make the connection between their polygynous system and their subsistence. When a missionary opposed to polygyny confronted the head of a large, multiple-wife household, the husband responded, "If I had only one or two wives I would starve; but with my present ten or twelve wives I can send them out in all directions in the morning and at least two or three of them are likely to bring something back with them at the end of the day, and then we can all eat." (Hart et al 1988:38)

The crucial importance of food gathering was a driving force behind the necessity for men who were starting their own households to begin by securing older widows as wives. It was older women who were experts in the environment and knew where to find food. Younger women acted as their apprentices, performing manual labor and learning all they could. While younger wives were important in that they could be counted on to provide infants to bestow, it was older women who were responsible for the household's standard of living. It was unusual for a household to begin in any other way than with a younger man and an older wife.

It is not surprising that older men were reported to be unendingly hostile toward the younger men in the camp. This was one consequence of a household structure in which elderly men had multiple wives, many of them young, while men in their twenties were unmarried, and those slightly older were married to elderly women. While this was economically quite efficient, it presented a social and "moral" problem. Older men had no difficulty in maintaining the food gathering and prestige enhancing facets of their households. It was a considerably greater challenge to keep young women who were out gathering every day away from young men who were at the same time out hunting. These purported daytime trysts gave rise to accusations hurled by older men to younger across the encampment fires nearly every night.

From all the foregoing, it would certainly seem that men and their interests are of sole importance in this system, with women being reduced to little more than pieces to be moved around a chessboard. Early ethnographic data collected among the Tiwi (and, for that matter, among most other groups) certainly reflected the perspectives of male ethnographers at this time. Regardless of the impressions given to an outsider, however, the Tiwi system functioned to the advantage of both men and women. Despite the early interpretations that made it appear favorable only to men, more recent ethnography among the Tiwi has allowed for reevaluation.

While male ethnographers have typically described Tiwi women primarily as wives, Serena Nanda (1991:236) suggests Tiwi men may be viewed as part

of the "fluctuating inventory" of women's husbands. Anthropologist Jane Goodale (1971) describes Tiwi women in just this manner.

Under the traditional system, a Tiwi girl became a mother-in-law as soon as she met the man who would marry any daughters she might bear. Her relationship to her prospective son-in-law was a very important one. He must provide both food and favors to his mother-in-law, and may join her camp at that time.

Regardless of the verbal jousting between older and younger men, Goodale (1971) reports that until a woman had her first pregnancy, she maintained both her sexual and social freedom, traditionally engaging in several extramarital unions with men her own age. This practice might not have been "officially" approved of, but was certainly acknowledged and tolerated. Once a woman gave birth to a girl, her son-in-law was thereafter expected to remain in his mother-in-law's service.

Power and prestige

As a woman progressed through her inevitable series of marriages, both her status and influence increased. In her role as manager of the household, an older woman was the linchpin of the Tiwi economy. As senior wife she was at the center of the powerful, cohesive social and economic unit which included her daughters and co-wives. In addition, she retained great influence over her sons. Goodale (1971) cautions us against the assumption that women in a polygynous society are by definition repressed by male authority. Tiwi woman have, in their solidarity with other women and their economic importance, both great power and great prestige.

Amassing the authority and eminence necessary to gain "big man" status among the Tiwi was a lifelong process. Influence was gained over decades of making alliances and currying favor. Since material goods were few (Hart et al 1988), prestige derived more from intangibles such as respect, control, friendship, and influence. One of the most important markers of success was a larder of food which could be given as gifts to individuals, or distributed at feasts. (Surplus food also afforded a man the leisure time to pursue social connections.)

Women were crucial in the acquisition of status for men, in that their labor was the vehicle for his amassing food surplus. As Hart et al (1988:58) summarize, "in the final analysis it was the control of women that was the most tangible index of power and influence. Women were the main currency of the influence struggle..."

As noted above, women, even in traditional Tiwi society, wielded considerable power, in part due to their centrality in the pursuit of big man status.

Power, for both men and women, came with age. Young Tiwi men had few assets and knew that they would have to wait many years for any return on an investment. Young Tiwi women were treated as property, "given away" as pawns in the strategy to gain influence. But older men had patiently amassed capital; older women had more control of their fate, and could not be coerced into joining a household unwillingly. Widows' decisions about which group to join in her subsequent marriage were effective instruments of power.

The complex systems of daughter bestowal and widow remarriage allowed young men to build the social alliances and food-surplus capital that would result in their elevation to big man status once they were elders.

RELIGION AND EXPRESSIVE CULTURE

Religious Beliefs

The Tiwi emphasize relationships between people far more than those between people and the supernatural. There are three worlds of existence: the world of the unborn, the world of the living, and the world of the dead. Each

individual passes through these three but once; each has a "life" in all three.

The world of the unborn--of the spirit children--is not one which is of much significance to Tiwi women. It figures greatly into the lives of Tiwi men, however, because it is men who "see" these children.

Earliest accounts (1959) reported that Tiwi recognize no biological contribution of a man to the conception of a child. Goodale (1971), in her pursuit of this line of questioning, was told in no uncertain terms that sexual intercourse with either a husband or a lover can result in pregnancy. However, this is a necessary but not sufficient contribution. In order for any Tiwi child to be conceived, it must be dreamed by its mother's husband.

Spirit children wait in their own world to be found by their parents. (When she asked what happens to those spirit children who were never found, Goodale was told that they married other unfound children, had children, grew old and died. That is, they lived out a complete life in the world of the unborn. [1971])

The spirit children inhabit the country owned by their potential father, and all the locations where these children are to be found are well known. Men see these children in their dreams, and they look human. They are playing in the sand, pretending to hunt, always wishing to be found. The ultimate goal of every spirit child is to be located and brought into the next world, that of the living.

The time spent in life is focused on personal achievement and economic independence. Children know that when they are very young or very old, they may be certain someone will see to their needs, care for them, provide them with food. They must learn enough about their environment to be able to be successful in operating within it for the majority of their time in this middle sphere of existence.

In the world of the dead, important relationships formed while alive are continued. Mothers live with their children, wives live with their husbands. All that one knows stays with them; all of ones talents are retained too. The world of the dead is the one static world. No one will move on to anyplace else, nor will they change in any way.

Tiwi religion revolves primarily around the taboos established for daily life; rituals involving death; and male initiation ceremonies. There is, conspicuous in its absence, none of the repertoire of "magical" means so commonly found elsewhere as a mechanism to deal with the unpredictability of the universe and the hostility of outsiders. Hart et al (1988) suggest there was no need to develop these beliefs in the benign Tiwi environment. Food and water were abundant; with the exception of snakes and crocodiles, the threat of wild animals was absent; there were few tropical diseases; natural disasters (such as earthquakes or hurricanes) were rare. Perhaps of singular importance was the absence of threatening neighbors. The isolation of the Tiwi resulted in their protection.

Taboo

The word "pukamani" is given both to a wide range of things seen as taboo as well as to the important funeral ceremony. In a generic sense, anything forbidden was pukamani, as were any people who, while not themselves "untouchable," were nonetheless in a ritually special state--such as in mourning, or having just given birth, or undergoing initiation rites. The overwhelming majority of circumstances surrounding pukamani have to do with death.

People who were in a pukamani state had elaborate sets of restrictions to follow, most often regarding food and sex. These requirements were not taken lightly, since the price generally exacted for their violation was failure in some desired enterprise. Ones prestige surely suffered when the explanation given for perpetual misfortune was breaking pukamani restrictions.

Religion had little to do with everyday Tiwi life, except as it related to pukamani observances, which were viewed not as active ways to petition spirits of effect change, but rather as obligations one undertook at certain times, quite out of ones own volition.

Kulama initiation ceremony

The annual kulama ceremony was one of the rare occasions (the other being funerals) necessitating that ordinarily dispersed households come together in joint activity. Because of the rarity of Tiwi gathering in large groups, the kulama was charged with excitement.

The kulama is a yam ceremony, part of the initiation into Tiwi adulthood. It is held each year at the end of the rainy season (March or April), and residents of a particular locale take part in the ceremony each year, passing through a series of named statuses. In addition to initiates, fully adult (that is, initiated) adults must participate in order to assure ones own good health, and that of ones children.

The ritual spans several days, beginning with the digging up of the kulama yam, a type not ordinarily consumed. Yams, which symbolize reproduction and health, are cooked and eventually eaten by the participants, who will attain the next kulama status at the completion of their participation.

Sickness and healing

It is the expectation of all Tiwi that they will live a long life, grow old, and die of old age. While they do recognize that illness or accident may strike, they still feel it is likely that they will one day be among the elderly.

Most unfortunate occurrences are thought to be brought upon the people by their own behavior, either in the form of breaking taboos, improper performance of ritual, or breach of social custom. The consequences of these infractions are varied: a hunter may have an accidental fall, or his eyesight grow dim. He may find not game, but a poisonous snake in his path. In most cases, Tiwi look no further than the individual for the source of the trouble. (Children's accidents are not subject to the same blame: they are the fault of the child's parent, whose laxity in teaching proper observation of rules is held to be the cause of a child's misfortune. It is not until children clearly know right from wrong that they can be held accountable.)

There are some occasions when bad luck, sickness, accidents, or even death are blamed on a spirit, but these are most certainly the exception. Sometimes the spirit of an individual will yearn so for a loved one, that it will send illness and death out of sheer loneliness and desire for a former companion.

In general, though, the responsibility for sickness is placed squarely at the feet of the person who is ill. This being the case, it is the patient who is the focus of the treatment, since he or she is, in effect, the causative agent. (This focus on the person as agent of illness or injury extends beyond self-blame; it is also imperative that individuals take responsibility for injury they have caused others. If one Tiwi injures another accidentally, the expected course of action is that the perpetrator will inflict the same injury on himself. When one dancer's spear accidentally cut another dancer's hand, the owner of the spear simply cut his own hand as an indication of its unintentional nature, and the dance continued uninterrupted, with nothing more said. [Goodale 1971])

The Tiwi have no ritual medical specialists. Healing is either first aid, or it is preventive medicine, and both categories are common knowledge.

Bloodletting and application of heat are considered effective in any illness, and frequently both are used in tandem. Burning sticks very effectively cauterize wounds, and the practice of bleeding the area around a snake bite is quite successful. The only "medicine" taken internally besides a potion of boiled grass was the drinking of the patient's own urine.

The prevention of illness is attended to much more assiduously than is treatment, since prevention is largely bound up with observance of taboo. Thus, the bulk of learning about illness prevention is actually contained in lessons about proper behavior.

Death and pukamani

When a person dies, the spirit rises up out of the body but does not travel far. After burial, the spirit hovers near the gravesite, making occasional visits to the camp to see loved ones still alive. In an attempt to convince the spirit to stay in the area of the grave, food, water and tobacco is left at the burial site, and the area around the grave is designated as hunting ground accessible only to that spirit. Although at first the spirit is very lonely for the people left behind, it gradually seeks companionship instead in the other spirits also residing at the burial grounds. Once fully accepting of the world of the dead, these spirits go on to have a "life" which is structured identically to the one left behind.

Spirits of the dead are generally believed to be invisible, but many individuals report having seen them. The sick are visited by spirits who tell them how long it will be until they will join the world of the dead. However, healthy people too have had occasion to happen upon these spirits.

Despite the close and loving relationship one might have had with a person before their death, once they are gone and only their spirit remains, the spirit is not to be trusted. This necessitates participation in certain rituals, aimed at showing the spirit that they are not forgotten, and at the same time beseeching it to be content with the new company it has found in the world of the dead, and to kindly let them continue living. On the first night after death, fires are built around the grave and kept burning all night. It is on this first night that the spirit will be loneliest, and most sorely tempted to come back for those left behind. The fires act as insurance that the spirits will be contained. (Accordingly, such elaborate precautions are not taken after the burial of an infant: this tiny spirit did not have a chance to know even its mother, and is not likely to want to come and claim any relative.)

The pukamani funeral ceremony is deemed the most important of a person's life. It is the individual who has died, not the mourners, who is the focus of the ceremony. Ones time in this middle world, the world of the living, cannot be finished until the completion of the funeral ceremony. Thus, although already dead, an individual's pukamani is still part of their life.

The pukamani, like the kulama initiation ceremony, brings Tiwi together in a gathering of unusual size. Unlike the kulama, however, which is organized to include only those who live within a circumscribed territory, the pukamani is intended to cast a much wider net. All those who have any sort of social tie with the deceased are expected to participate, making it the only event in Tiwi life (with the possible exception of full-scale warfare) that is organized around such a varied group. This event demands an unusual degree of organization to prevent utter chaos, especially since the entire process will last several days. Participants are divided into groups based on their kin ties. Individuals from among a group of leaders, also determined by kinship, are each assigned responsibility for a segment of the assemblage. Ritual behaviors are also prescribed based on ones affiliation with the deceased, adding an additional element of structure. The actual degree of contact the participants have had with the deceased on a daily basis is not at issue: ritual tasks are assigned by membership in certain social categories (for example, "close kin" versus "long-way kin.").

Ordinarily, a person's close family will be in attendance at the time of death, and it is these individuals who must observe the most stringent taboos: they become "pukamani." While the very young and very old are exempt from these requirements (because some are considered too strenuous), all others who are close consanguineal or affinal kin living in the camp must conform.

Immediately following the death, those who are pukamani smear white clay over the entire surface of their bodies, including

their face and hair. The surviving spouse will have his or her hair cut close to the scalp; men shave their beards. This will be done again at the conclusion of the mourning period. These outward signs display ones entry into the pukamani state, and often the clay is not washed off for the entire duration of the ceremonies. They may, in fact, be repainted each day, with elaborate designs added.

Once burial has taken place, all women who are pukamani tear pandanus leaves into strips and weave armbands to be worn along the entire length of both arms by men and women who are also pukamani. The number of armbands worn varies by the degree of closeness to the deceased. These are painted over as the daily clay is added, incorporating them into the design as if they were bare skin. The painting and armbands serve to at once hide and identify: living Tiwi will see they are pukamani; spirits of the dead will not recognize them. (A murderer will paint himself after the crime--as if he were a mourner and not the assailant--to escape the vengeance of his victim's spirit.)

Once painted, those who are pukamani begin a period of severely circumscribed behavior which may last several months. They may not be close to any source of water (which may explain why they do not wash one body painting off before applying the next), and cannot touch their own food. Their meals must be fed to them; even water must be lifted to their lips, as they cannot touch even the containers in which their food and drink are served. Sexual intercourse is forbidden.

The taboos established by death go well beyond the actions immediately restricted for close kin. Everything owned by the deceased becomes taboo. Many items are brought to the gravesite and placed atop the burial mound. Once so situated, they are not to be touched, lest they cause illness. The purpose in removing these belongings is to remove the sadness that would be engendered for the mourners were they to see these things again. Large and valuable items (such as canoes or tools) can be inherited by women and men close to the deceased, after they have been ritually cleansed by "smoking," (a process much like curing meat) which repels the spirit of the dead.

Items which have been touched by the deceased are also taboo, and anyone who handled them would swell up and die. Special care is taken not to place food in any container previously belonging to the deceased.

The name of the deceased, along with the names he bestowed on others, and any words that sound like the name of the deceased, become taboo. (This led to a crisis when a man named Tibuki died, preventing Tiwi in the area from requesting tobacco at the local mission: the similarity in sounds made the word pukamani. [Hart et al 1988]) The name of the surviving spouse is similarly pukamani, thus he or she must instead be referred to by the terms for widow or widower, rather than either a proper name or nickname.

The preparation for the elaborate pukamani ceremony begins with messengers sent out to announce the death in all the regions where there are kin who must attend. These messengers paint themselves bright red, and carry special message sticks. Thus attired, he is noticeable at quite a distance, and a crowd gathers to hear whose death has occurred. When the death is announced, relatives of the deceased fall into each others arms and weep.

Singing and dancing figure prominently into the pukamani ceremony, and Tiwi can gain great prestige for their prowess as composer and performer. Songs usually center around mythological or historical themes, with items of current events woven through. (Much to Goodale's horror, as she listened to a "modern" pukamani song during a return trip to the Islands, and asked for an explanation of the text--which sounded suspiciously like it had been inspired by a movie depicting the old Wild West-- she was told, "Why, it's [about the cowboy] Hopalong [Cassidy] and the Indians, you should know that!" [1971:294])

Dancing sometimes becomes frenzied with grief, resulting in performers beating and cutting themselves. This is most often done as a display by people who are not close relatives of the deceased, in order to "join" in the grief of those who are pukamani. Goodale (1971) suggests that this is reminiscent of the "guilty" self-inflicted cuts which serve as displays of remorse after accidentally injuring another.

Perhaps the best known feature of the pukamani ceremony are the carved and brightly painted poles are set up around the gravesite. Both the shaping and painting of the poles are done with elaborate intricacy, with no two alike. Since the poles represent the status and prestige of the deceased, great pains are taken to ensure the creation of the most beautiful and complicated poles possible.

At the conclusion of the mourning period, those about to leave the pukamani state wash off their clay body painting, rip off the panadanus armbands, and throw them on top of the grave.

MODERN TIWI LIFE

In the eighty years since the first anthropologists visited Melville and Bathurst Islands, much has changed. In the 1920s Japanese pearlers were active; by the 1940s Catholic missions were exerting great influence. The Islands did not escape involvement in World War II, victims of bombing and strafing by Japanese war planes.

By the conclusion of the war, Tiwi had become largely dependent upon the products supplied to them by military bases, and most settled near a Catholic mission on Bathurst Island. Polygamous marriages, traditionally the cornerstone of so much of Tiwi social and economic structure, were outlawed. This policy was put into effect by missionaries who "purchased" young women, and then "allowed" them to select a single mate from among their own age group. (Hart et al 1988) By the 1950s many young Tiwi women had been converted to Christianity, and did not wish to share their households with co-wives.

Residence patterns were altered dramatically as nearly all Tiwi lived in one of four European sites with centralized village patterns. By the early 1950s, polygamous households had all but disappeared. Rather than adopting the nuclear family of the Europeans, Tiwi maintained large households of extended families. While there was only one wife, older widowed women were taken into the home to care for the children while younger women went out to gather food.

Perhaps the most significant change concerning native Australian peoples was the return of ownership of their land under the Land Rights Act of 1976. The Tiwi thus became owners once again of Melville and Bathurst Islands, establishing the Tiwi Land Council with elected representatives from each of the traditional "countries."

Contemporary Tiwi society is very much a part of the modern world system. Tourism and industry organized around the selling of indigenous Tiwi art has become an important part of the Tiwi's economic base. However, they remain active hunters and gatherers, and the traditional kulama and pukamani ceremonies endure. These may be less elaborate in form, but retain all the most fundamental elements.

After many years of "development" by outsiders, the Tiwi are now faced with the determination of their own future, as they were in the past. Returning to the Islands in the late 1980s, anthropologist Goodale observed that in the development of their tourist trade, Tiwi retained their noncommercial perspective. They embrace the challenge of balancing their desire to keep traditional culture alive for their children, while aspiring to participate in the global economy.

REFERENCES

GOODALE, J.C.
  1971   *Tiwi Wives*. Seattle: University of Washington Press.

HART, C.W.M., A. R. PILLING, AND J.C.GOODALE
  1988   *The Tiwi of North Australia.* New York: Holt, Rinehart & Winston

§ THE BEGINNING

One of the ancestors shot Moon in the belly. Moon's blood fell on the earth, and the drops of blood became people, people who were fierce. The blood that was thickest became the people who were most warlike, and they nearly killed each other in their hostility. Where the blood mixed with water and was thinner, the drops made people who fought less. This is why people are so fierce. (Chagnon 1992)

INTRODUCTION: THE YANOMAMO ENVIRONMENT

The Yanomamo are a tribe of 20,000 who live in about 250 widely dispersed villages in Brazil and Venezuela. Although they are well-known to students of anthropology, owing largely to the lifelong study of Napoleon Chagnon, they have remained remarkably isolated and undisturbed until very recently. Theirs is a history of very little contact and retention of indigenous patterns, although the impact of recent interference has been dramatic.

The tropical forest in which the Yanomamo live is dense and green, with varied growth. Its thick floor of vines and scrub make it difficult to traverse; on cloudy days its impenetrable canopy keeps out most light.

Villages are at varying distances from one another, and have differing degrees of social closeness as well. Those which harbor good relations host frequent visitors. Others are engaged in the warfare for which the Yanomamo are well known.

SUBSISTENCE AND MANUFACTURE

Gardening and foraging

The earliest reports about the Yanomamo erroneously described them as hunters and gatherers. Chagnon (1992) postulates that this was based on the assumption that a tribe as isolated as the Yanomamo could not possibly possess the sophistication to be cultivators.

In fact, the abundant jungle could easily provide for the complete diet of a foraging group, and Yanomamo do exploit the wild foods found in their environment. However, although the wild resources could support the Yanomamo, utilizing them would necessitate a different lifestyle: that of a small, mobile band. While the Yanomamo travel for several weeks when the jungle fruits and vegetables are ripe, they are a tribal society settled in villages, which break into small groups to go off on collecting expeditions. Honey is the ultimate wild prize, and honeycombs are often consumed with the larvae still inside.

Game is plentiful too, and during these expeditions they commonly hunt wild pigs, large and small birds, monkeys, deer, rodents, and anteaters. Armadillos, who live in underground burrows, cannot be hunted with bow and arrow. They are ingeniously smoked out. Once an entry to a burrow is located, a slow smoky fire is lit. Smoke escaping from other burrows indicate exits to be dammed up. Once all escape routes are blocked, hunters listen with an ear to the ground for the scurrying of the animal, and dig straight down to retrieve it. Insects and shellfish round out the protein portion of their diet.

Fish do not provide an extensive portion of the Yanomamo diet, but when the rainy season is over and pools formed by overflowing rivers dry out, stranded fish can be opportunistically gathered by women. This practice includes the use of mild poisons, introduced into the water upstream. The drugged fish float to the surface where they are easily grabbed and tossed into baskets. Larger fish who are less stunned by the poison are bitten behind the head by the women and killed.

The bulk of Yanomamo food (more than eighty percent) is grown in their village gardens. Garden sites are cleared by cutting down trees and brush and burning them, although not with the systematic precision of other slash-and-burn-practitioners. Large tree trunks which have been felled but are too wet to burn are simply left where they fall, and either used as firewood once dry, or allowed to serve as boundary markers between the gardens of different families.

The size of a garden plot is usually dictated by the size of the family it must feed. Since village headmen will have the responsibility of entertaining visitors and sponsoring feasts, they plant and care for larger plots.

Plantain is the most important domesticated crop. Manioc, taro, and sweet potato are also cultivated. Cane used in arrow manufacture is grown in village gardens, as is tobacco, a crop of central importance. All women, men, and children chew it daily and guard it jealously. Chagnon (1992) reports that it is the only crop that is fenced off to warn potential thieves. The value of tobacco (to which every Yanomamo above the age of ten is reportedly addicted) is evidenced by the fact that the local word for being "poor" is literally "without tobacco." (Chagnon 1992)

Cotton grown in village gardens is used predominantly for the construction of hammocks, an item owned by everyone. It is also used to make what little clothing is worn. Men typically wear little more than a string around the waist, while more ornate belts are generally worn by the women. Single strands of cotton string are also tied around wrists and ankles.

Manufacture

The technology found among the Yanomamo is not complex. Any necessary tool can be manufactured from materials readily available in any village. The knowledge of how to do so is widely held. The level of manufacture has been compared to that of typical foraging societies, despite the fact that they are horticulturalists. (Chagnon 1992)

Palm wood is used to make numerous items, among them bows and arrow points. One type of palm wood arrow point that is highly prized is one used in hunting with curare, a poison extracted from a local vine. The point is dipped in curare and shaved to insure that it will break off underneath the skin, preventing the victim from removing it. The curare, which induces muscle relaxation, is then sent into the bloodstream. Poison arrow tips are among the most popular items of trade between villages. Quivers which hold them are made from bamboo, and are worn hanging on the back. Arrows themselves are fashioned from cane, and are quite long, resembling spears.

Other manufactured items include large shallow baskets used to collect fish, and a rudimentary "razor," used to create the Yanomamo's unique haircut, bowl-shaped with a circle shaved bald at the top center of the head. This is the style worn by both men and women. The exception is during an exceptionally severe bout with head lice, when it is simply easier to completely shave the heads of affected men, women, and children .

Village construction

Houses are constructed from readily available local materials, predominantly saplings for support posts, vines, and leaves for thatching. These are not very durable, despite the substantial labor which goes into their construction. In addition to being little protection against rains, after only a year or two, the leafy roofs become so infested with insects that there is no other option but to burn them and start again. (Chagnon comments that roaches often grow to the size of small birds. [1992])

Living space, called the shabono, is a series of individual homes, sheltered underneath a common roof. Men sink the four main posts into the ground, and woman and children gather the vines and leaves used for thatching. Thousands of these leaves are needed to cover the structure. Each family builds the section of the roof that covers their own compartment. When the structure is complete, there are numerous individual sections with a few feet between them, all underneath a long stretch of connected thatching, surrounding an open central plaza. The building site is chosen with an eye to the suitability of the surrounding land for gardening, as well as proximity to both allies and enemies.

If there is continual threat of enemy attack, a tall wooden fence is constructed behind the shabono. The fence is covered with dry brush at night, so that intruders will be heard by village dogs, who will in turn wake the residents.

Village size will, of course, reflect the size of the population, which may be as small as forty or as large as three hundred. But another factor determining size is the number of neighboring villages with whom friendly relations are maintained. It is important to be able to accommodate any allies who will be visiting regularly. Thus, a village size may reflect not the number of permanent residents, but the number of people it will have to house when visitors are expected.

To house visitors or to provide shelter on extended food gathering forays less elaborate temporary shelter are constructed. These are usually made by lashing three poles together and covering them with broad banana leaves.

RELIGION AND EXPRESSIVE CULTURE

The relatively simple technology and material culture of the Yanomamo is not replicated in their systems of belief and expression. Although they have no tradition of writing, their use of language is elegant and verbal skills are highly prized.

The Yanomamo envision the universe as being constructed of four layers hovering atop one another with a thin layer of space between them. The topmost strata is empty, and has least to do with current Yanomamo life. Long ago, things may have come from here, but now it lies fallow. The layer below it is the sky. People can only see its underside, onto which stars are stuck, but the surface of the sky is believed to look much as the earth does, with trees and plants and animals. The most important residents of this layer are the souls of the dead, who carry on an existence there much like the one they had as living Yanomamo. This layer--the sky--is believed to float quite close to the earth, as Chagnon (1992) deduced from the repeated questioning about bumping into it when he flew in airplanes.)

The third layer down, on which the Yanomamo live, was created when a section of the "sky" layer cracked off and toppled down. The bottommost layer, which exists under the earth, was formed when sky fell to earth on top of a particular settlement, and pushed it down through the earth to the underside. There it has settled as the last layer, along with the people, their homes and garden. Unfortunately, their hunting grounds were left behind. Loss of the jungle in which to find game led them inevitably to cannibalism, and the unfortunate souls of Yanomamo children are their usual prey. The belief that souls are regularly carried off to be eaten down below reflects the Yanomamo's fear that natives of the earth can indeed fall into the practice of cannibalism,. This possibility apparently both terrifies and disgusts them. Chagnon (1992) elaborates: "Whenever I hunted with them and we shot a tapir, I would always cut off a thick juicy slice of tenderloin and fry it lightly on both sides-- a rare steak that dripped juicy delicious blood as I cut it and ate it. This so disgusted and alarmed them that they could not bear to watch me eat it, and invariably accused me of wanting to become a cannibal... a disgusting eater of raw flesh. For their part, they cook their meat so much that you could almost drive nails with it." (pp 101-2).

These dwellers of the bottom layer of the universe were in existence when the first people originated. Those original human beings were different from people today in that they were part human, part animal, and part spirit. When they died, they became all spirit--the hekura who figure prominently into Yanomamo shamanism.

Myths

Many Yanomamo myths are built around these original humans, called "those who are now dead." Although tales of their origin are spotty, they themselves are responsible for the creation of many plants and animals, and are in fact the spirits of those living things which bear their names.

Men are generally the storytellers in Yanomamo society, and they "perform" the recounting of a myth more than simply recite them. Their histrionic style, often enhanced by drugs, leads to dramatic embellishments and provides enjoyable diversion for the audience.

Some stories incorporate a moral, designed to teach the ways of Yanomamo. Others are told to explain why the world is as it is. Many are sheer entertainment.

The relationship of humankind to the jaguar is a theme which predominates in many stories. Chagnon (1992) suggests that the jaguar may have been chosen because it effectively exemplifies a fundamental theme in Yanomamo culture, (and many others) the distinction between "nature" and "culture." Jaguar is in some ways a figure in which nature and culture overlap. The Yanomamo are proud that humans have culture and animals do not. Yet Jaguar is a hunter as skilled as a Yanomamo. He hunts not only animals but people, as the Yanomamo do. Jaguar is an animal--a creature of nature--who shares traits with people--bearers of culture--and is both feared and respected. In many of their jaguar stories, the fierce and powerful jaguar is reduced to a clumsy inefficient beast. In the creation of these stories, culture triumphs over nature.

The Yanomamo soul

The soul plays a central part in the "spiritual" world of the Yanomamo. It is the soul which is consumed by the cannibals in the netherworld, and it is a rather sophisticated "organ."

The soul consists of several different portions, each of which has a function in both life and death. The part of the soul which is the "will," is the part that makes the journey to the afterlife. At death, it shimmies up the ropes of the deceased's hammock, entering the layer of the universe above the earth, and begins a journey down a road which divides into two separate paths. This fork is guarded by a spirit, who is charged with assessing the generosity shown by the soul's mortal owner during its life, and then sending it down the appropriate path. Generous souls are directed down the path to the comfortable earth-like place; stingy ones are shepherded down the fork to a fiery place. (This latter fate is not one which causes them great worry: they are unimpressed by the intelligence of the guard, and plan simply to lie and be sent down the preferred route.)

There is another part of the soul that is freed upon cremation of the body, and lives thereafter in the jungle. This portion has the potential for evil, clubbing people who visit the jungle at night. Great caution is exercised to avoid them.

The most crucial portion of the Yanomamo soul resides within the chest or flank (interestingly, that portion of the body attacked in stylized chest- and side-pounding duels), and is most vulnerable to attack. This component can be stolen, and then subject to supernatural attack. If this happens, the individual sickens and will likely die unless this portion of the soul is restored.

The last aspect of the soul lives both inside and outside the individual. Inside, it is a part of the individual spirit (the part captured by the camera when a person is photographed); outside it is a person's animal counterpart, which leads a parallel life. When the person eats, his or her animal-self is doing the same. When the person is asleep, so too is the animal. Ordinarily one will never meet this animal alter ego, but if by some twist of fate one were to hunt and kill it, ones own death would follow (as it does when another hunter kills "your animal.")

ILLNESS, HEALING, AND DEATH

Illness is caused by the hekura spirits which harm a person by consuming a portion of their soul, usually at the behest of someone from an enemy village. It is the charge of a shaman to call upon his own powerful hekura to counterattack, thus curing the sick villager.

Shamanism is a practice open only to Yanomamo men. However, it is not a role restricted by birth or special characteristics or suitabilities. Anyone who wishes may undertake the training, if they are willing to undergo the rigors entailed. These include a fast which may last up to a year, during which the initiate becomes emaciated. Instructors, who are older shamans, guide the novices in the ways to call their own hekura spirits to them. They must learn the likes and dislikes of the hekura, in order to lure them into ones chest. This is not an easy task--they are difficult to seduce, and apt to be fickle and leave abruptly. An aspiring shaman must endeavor to make the interior of his body into attractive terrain in which the hekura may dwell in comfort. If they find verdant mountains and cool streams in the shamans chest, they may stay. Older, more proficient shamans may have succeeded in attracting many hekura spirits to live within them, yet are always striving to keep them happy. Since hekura are repelled by sexual activities, younger novices have no hope of attracting and keeping the hekura unless they are celibate. This requirement alone often deters men from the pursuit of this status. Once a shaman has established a stable relationship with the hekura, he may engage in sex without fear of abandonment by his spiritual powers.

Hekura, who dwell among the Yanomamo in the thousands, are both male and female, but all are exceedingly beautiful. Different sorts have different temperaments. The most fearsome are the "hot and meat hungry" hekura, for these are the ones who devour the souls of enemies.

Shamans have access to the hekura only while they are under the influence of hallucinogens. These drugs are used on a daily basis, and their preparation is ongoing. They are ingested in powder form, blown into the nose through a long hollow pipe placed in the mouth of another man. The initial effects are quite painful, leading to coughing, choking, watery eyes, and retching. Their power takes effect almost immediately. As the shamans begin to feel intoxicated, they begin their chanting, which calls their hekura to them. Since the hekura are themselves so beautiful, they require great attractiveness on the part of the shaman, who wear feathers and paint themselves elaborately. Once the hekura have danced down their trails and into the chests of their hosts, they can aid a shaman in curing They can also be manipulated to go to enemy villages and avenge the sickness sent on local villagers.

When a Yanomamo dies, the body is cremated. This is done by carrying the body to a prepared pile of firewood, where it is burned. One person is designated to watch the fire, making sure hat the entire corpse is consumed, and nothing but ash and bone remains. A log is hollowed out to hold the teeth and bones, which are ground by a close kinsman and apportioned into several small gourds. Any ashes remaining in the log's hollow are consumed in soup, and then the log is burned. The gourds full of ashes are kept for a larger more elaborate ceremony during which they will be added to more soup and consumed by visiting kin from other villages.

If there are multiple deaths occurring at one time, all the bodies are taken into the jungle. Rather than being burned, they are wrapped with bark and positioned in trees until they decompose. Later the remaining bones are burned, and the same ash-drinking ceremony takes place.

SOCIAL ORGANIZATION

Leadership

Each Yanomamo village has a headman, an individual who usually belongs to the largest kin group represented in the village. He serves more as a representative of his own village in dealings with other villages than as a authoritarian figure within his own. Chagnon (1992), who in his visits to more than sixty Yanomamo villages has seen the leadership styles of many headmen, reports that there is no one personality that typifies this status. Some headmen are quiet, introspective leaders; others are bombastic and dictatorial. What they have in common is the limitations inherent in the status afforded them. They act as hosts and negotiators. Their opinions carry somewhat more weight. They lead by example and not by decree. If there is trouble within the village, it is the headman's responsibility to attempt to restore order. Since he must model the behavior he wishes others to exhibit, his life is often fraught with more risks. He demonstrates the bravery, or self-control, or industriousness that he expects others to display.

Male and female

The realities of daily life differ greatly for Yanomamo men and women. Chagnon (1992) calls it "decidedly masculine," and this certainly seems borne out in the ethnographic information he provides.

Girls are aware at an early age that they have far less social room in which to maneuver than do their brothers. They begin to assume a productive role in their household at a very early age, and assume childcare responsibilities while they are themselves small children.

Most girls are betrothed while they are still quite young, and they have no opportunity to voice any preference (or register any dissent) in this regard. The men to whom they are promised are usually much older. In some cases, they identify girl and ask their relatives to make marriage inquiries. She may then be "raised" to some extent by the man who is to become her husband. Regardless of the age at which she is promised, girls do not generally take up residence with their husbands until reaching puberty.

Even when their marriage "officially" begins, life changes little for a Yanomamo girl. She continues to spend her days as she has previously done: collecting firewood, cooking, and devoting herself to the needs of others around her. One aspect of her marital relationship which does appear to be unique to the husband-wife dyad is the physical cruelty to which Yanomamo women are subjected by their husbands. According to Chagnon this is commonplace and expected behavior. Women are physically disciplined by their husbands for a host of "infractions," ranging from being to slow to prepare a meal to suspected infidelity. Punishment runs the gamut from blows with firewood or axes, burns, arrow wounds to murder. Women often depend on their brothers to protect them from an "unusually" cruel husband, and despair of being promised to a man in another village where they will separated from this potential source of protection.

While women appear to gain no status from the transition from single girl to married woman, they are afforded more respect and fear less for their safety as they age. Elderly women can travel even between warring villages without fearing harm, which is more than they can be assured in their own homes when they are young wives.

Boys are socialized early into this behavior through the encouragement they receive to strike others, especially little girls, when they are angry. Boys as young as four or five are well aware of their license to "[inflict] blows ... on the hapless girls in the village" (Chagnon 1992:126), and are cheered on by their parents and others who often goad them into this behavior during play.

"Play" lasts nearly twice as long for boys as it does for girls. While a girl of 10 spends the bulk of her day as a worker, boys in their late teens may still be enjoying childhood. This often causes difficulties, because boys of this age expend much effort attempting to seduce girls of their own age--who are generally married women, often with several children.

Children--both boys and girls--are particularly susceptible to malevolent spirits, often sent from enemy villages to attack their souls. They are vulnerable in this fashion because their souls are not yet moored securely within their bodies. Young souls, given to wandering, escape from the mouth when a child cries.

POLITICAL AND ECONOMIC ORGANIZATION

Forging alliances

The focus of "political" life among the Yanomamo centers on forging and maintaining ties between villages. There are several ways in which alliances may be formed.

Inherent in these ties is the obligation to offer asylum to residents of an allied village who are fleeing an enemy. Since leaving ones village means leaving ones garden--hence, ones economic base--it is sometimes necessary for this "visit" to be quite lengthy. Guests will stay in a village while they are establishing a new garden in a safer site. Chagnon (1992) observed more than one occasion when an enemy's capture of a village led to the displaced Yanomamo to rely on the hospitality of an allied village for a year or more. Such an imposition exacts a commensurate cost, and payment is usually demanded in women. The other options open to an invaded group are only either standing ground and attempting to withstand the hostile onslaught, or dispersing into small family units and joining other villages permanently. Neither of these is preferable to the pattern of "visiting" for only as long as it takes to establish a new garden elsewhere, and then moving on.

With the threat of attacking always looming, no village can afford to be without the alliances that insure they will have somewhere to go after invasion. Chagnon (1992) points out an inherent conflict in the need to forge alliances as protection against attack: warfare among the Yanomamo is predicated on the belief that stronger villages should overpower weaker ones. This encourages villages to present as strong a face to outsiders as they possibly can. This posture is difficult to maintain while engaging in the development of dependent friendships. He summarizes, "Allies *need* but cannot really *trust* each other." (p. 160)

Trade relations and feasting are the usual channels for creating ties between villages, but the most secure alliances are formed by marriage. Not all relations between villages proceed to this final step, because the mistrust always beneath the surface in intervillage relations leads Yanomamo to suspect the promise of reciprocity. In fact, it is only the minority of villages that progress past the arguments and accusations about women that are produced in the course of trading and feasting, prerequisites for marital exchange.

Trading

Trade between Yanomamo villages follows a pattern which is self-propelling; that is, rules are established such that trade leads to more trade.

All items traded must be reciprocated with an item of a different sort. Usually these are representative of the "specialty" of the village. The return gift must be presented in the proper time frame. It cannot be immediately exchanged. The former feature serves as an "excuse" to continue trading with a particular village. One village doesn't usually possess a resource or skill which is unique. However, claiming that ties are being maintained with another village solely because it guarantees access to a needed item functions as a face-saving mechanism. It allows interdependence --in

the form of repeated visiting to trade for the specialty item--without demonstrating weakness. The element of elapsed time results in an ongoing relationship of indebtedness: one village always owes payment to the other.

Chagnon (1992) points out that these explanations for the "ulterior motives" of trading and feasting are not ones which the Yanomamo themselves readily volunteer. Outwardly, they never say "we must maintain these ties so that we can call upon them during times of war." Feasts and trading expeditions are ends in and of themselves. Likewise, the hosts of such events seize the opportunity to demonstrate their power and wealth, without overtly expressing the fact that it places them in a position of strength.

Feasting

Feasts among the Yanomamo are usually much-anticipated occasions for both hosts and guests. They are an opportunity to eat, drink, and flirt; to display oneself proudly; and to affirm and deepen ties of mutuality. Given the constant undercurrent of defensiveness and opportunism, however, there is always the potential for something going awry and culminating in violence.

Men take the primary responsibility for preparing food for feasts. Since one hundred or more guests may be expected, hunting, gathering, and cooking is a large-scale task. Although a messenger is sent to the guest village with an invitation only on the day of the feast, preparation at the host village starts long before.

Game meat and plantain are the main foodstuffs which are served, and large quantities of plantain are harvested and hung to ripen in anticipation. Many of these will be used to make soup, cooked in large strips of bark which is cut and fashioned into troughs of sufficient size to hold up to one hundred gallons of soup.

A hunting party is organized to secure meat, and as the hunters set off, the excitement surrounding a feast begins to build. When they return, the meat is presented to the headman, smoked at his fire, and wrapped for later presentation.

Both village and villagers are groomed for the festivities. The central village clearing is weeded and swept to prepare it for dancing. Houses are neatened and scraps from the preparation of food and gifts are disposed of. Both men and women paint their faces and bodies and decorate themselves with bright feathers. Men further prepare by ingesting hallucinogenic drugs. Guests are adorning themselves similarly, in anticipation of their formal parade into the center of the host village.

As the guest delegated to begin the processional enters the village, appreciative cheers erupt from the hosts. There is a formality in this presentation: he is elaborately painted and festooned with parrot feathers and monkey tails. Reaching the center of the clearing, he stops and strikes a predictable posture: standing still, haughty, weapons in the "visitor's pose" by his face. He maintains this stance for several minutes. He is there to be admired; but he is also there to express his peaceful intent. With his weapons held, motionless and fully exposed, he declares himself to be without hostility and invites an easy shot if malice is contemplated.

This accomplished, he approaches the designated host (the village headman or his representative) and the two begin a chant which signifies the acceptance of the invitation by the guests, and officially initiates the feast. Spirited and at the top of their voices, the two dance and chant for five or ten minutes, and the guest departs to arrange the formal entry of his village.

Guests assemble at the entryway, with the men in front, and women and children holding gifts behind the front ranks. At their headman's signal, visiting dancers spring into the village in pairs, whirling and chanting along the edge of the central plaza, and then returning to the rest of the group, still outside the village walls. Each man enters the village in this manner, displaying his own unique body painting, chant, and aggressive facial expression. When everyone has a chance to do this, attended all the while by the enthusiastic

cheers and whoops of their hosts, the assembled group enters, one by one, dancing along the rim of the clearing, coming to a halt in the center of the plaza where they stood for silent inspection.

One by one, hosts approach the throng of guests and lead each family unit off to his own house. As the guests eat their first serving of plantain soup, the host men gather their village to make a formal entrance and display of their own decoration.

From dusk to dawn, all are engaged in chanting and trading. Visitors tell their headmen which items they want; this request is relayed to the host headman, who entreats one of his villagers to provide it. Once presented, it is inspected by the recipient and his friends, who praise it even as the donor apologizes for its obvious inadequacies. (Unless it is, in fact, truly inadequate. Then, the presenter calls attention to all its finer attributes, while the recipient points out each flaw.) In any case, the hosts always claim to have given more than they should; guests always assert they have been undercompensated. Bickering accompanied every trade.

Should arguing escalate, for any of a number of reasons, such as impoliteness, intimidation, and the exchange of insults, a chest-pounding duel may ensue. The entry into the host village to signify the acceptance of such a challenge bears little resemblance to that which begins a feast. Guests arrive waving their axes, clubs, bows and arrows. They are received with the noises made by hosts clattering their arrows together and thumping clubs and arrows on the ground as they surround the guests, each host selecting the guest they will fight.

A chest-pounding duel is not a spontaneous brawl. The blows delivered are carefully calculated and stylized. One partner presents himself, daring the other to hit him. The recipient of the challenge assesses the position struck, realigns his victim's arms or chest so they can be most effectively pounded. He measures and remeasures the distance he wants his arm to be from the victim's chest, feinting several trial punches. Finally, "he

...[winds] up like a baseball pitcher...and [delivers] a tremendous wallop with his fist to the man's [chest], putting all of his weight into the blow." (Chagnon 1992:179) The victim, reeling from the punch, is urged on by his fellows not to back down, but to present himself for another blow. A maximum of four blows may be struck before victim and aggressor change places. Each aggressor is required to return the same number of poundings as he receives. Only if severely injured in his receipt of the retaliatory blows may a victim withdraw from the fight after receiving fewer hits than he has inflicted. Fighting may continue in this vein for several hours, often with many agitating for its escalation to the use of axes. While headmen often oppose this, knowing it will lead to bloodshed, there is a variation on the chest-slapping duel, "side" slapping, to which it sometimes escalates. This open-handed smacking of the opponents side between rib cage and pelvis often incurs greater injury, especially when a fistful of stones replaces an open hand. While chest-pounding blows are directed to the muscular portion of the chest, there is no such protection of the organs beneath blows to the flank. In one fight witnessed by Chagnon (1992), two young men died after a side-slapping fight, most likely due to ruptured kidneys. (Death occurs after chest-pounding too, and it is not uncommon that participants cough up blood for several days after these confrontations.)

YANOMAMO VIOLENCE AND WARFARE

As is evidenced by the outright choreography of the chest-pounding duel, many forms of fighting among the Yanomamo are strictly regulated. The aggression so assiduously cultivated in males is released in these formalized duels, as an attempt to avoid warfare.

A step up from the chest-pounding and side-slapping duels is attacks with clubs, often the result of arguments over women and food. These are not restricted to outsiders: co-villagers can and do attack each other with clubs. Chagnon (1992) tells of an incident in which a father clubbed his son for eating some of the older man's bananas without permission. The son retaliated with his own club, and soon most of the men in the village had taken up the cause of one side or the other.

The clubs are actually heavy 10 foot long poles. One end is sharpened to a point, allowing it to be turned and used as a spear should it be necessary. The most common scenario for the instigation of club fights is the accusation made by a husband that another man has been carrying on an affair with his wife. The jealous husband grabs his pole, and after accusing the other man, presents his own head to be hit. Once the accused succumbs to the challenge and strikes him, the husband may retaliate. As the first blood is drawn, much of this orchestration falls away. Most observers will yank a pole out of the framework of the house and join in the fight, soon to have blood streaming down their heads and necks.

It is not surprising that the tops of most male Yanomami heads boast a network of deep scars. Some of the men who keep the top central portion of their heads shaved do so to proudly display the impressive thick knots they have received in club fights.

Since larger villages afford more opportunity for adultery, they also are plagued with more club fighting. As sides are taken, often along kinship lines, large villages sometimes split in two over these confrontations.

An escalation to the next level leads to raids, which are considered true warfare. The objective is usually to kill as many of the enemy as possible, and escape undetected. However, if any of the attacking group are killed, the raid is considered a failure, regardless of the number of enemies dispatched before one of the invaders was killed.

During the course of a raid on an enemy village, women are often abducted. This, however, is not usually the objective around which the raid is organized, but rather a "side benefit" of a successful endeavor. In villages with acute shortages of women, wars have been initiated for the sole intent of capturing them. One such war is an example of nomohori ("dastardly trick"), the ultimate form of treachery and violence. Raiders arrived at a distant village, saying they acquired machetes and cooking pots through prayer to a previously unknown spirit. The raiders offered to teach the unsuspecting villagers this prayer, so that they too could receive the goods. As the men knelt down and bowed their heads, preparing to be instructed in prayer, the raiders hacked them to death with their machetes, captured the women of the village and fled. (Chagnon 1992)

Once villages are already at war with one another, stealing women is a common occurrence in ongoing raids. New conflicts are more likely to arise out of an accusation of sorcery or food theft.

YANOMAMO: CHANGING CULTURE

Life for the Yanomamo is changing. Contact with Catholic missionaries began many years ago in some villages. In others direct contact has yet to occur. Groups of Yanomamo whose lives remain relatively unchanged from their traditional patterns are few, and becoming fewer.

Some of the most dramatic consequences are a result of the 1987 gold rush in Brazil, which brought not only miners with guns and heavy machinery, but previously unencountered diseases, which indigenous peoples could not withstand. The Yanomamo in Venezuela have been less affected, but are still endangered. There has been intervention by the government in these nations. The United States is considering altering their foreign aid policy, such that moneys are contingent upon the proper treatment of indigenous peoples.

Anthropologist Napoleon Chagnon, after a career invested so heavily in the Yanomamo people, has devoted extensive efforts to their protection, and the task of safeguarding the rights and cultures of other indigenous groups. He writes, "The Yanomamo are now a symbol for all tribesman everywhere, perhaps the ultimate test case of whether ordinary concerned, educated and determined people can stay a destructive process that will [otherwise] be inevitable." (1992:246)

REFERENCE

CHAGNON, N.
    1992   *Yanomamo*. Fort Worth:
                Harcourt Brace
                Jovanovich.